# History of the Wars by Prc

## The Vandalic War.  Books III & IV

Procopius of Caesarea was born in approximately 500. He is generally considered to be the last major historian of the ancient world. His works have given us a unique and intimate account both of the Roman Military and its Emperor Justinian.

A native of Caesarea in Palaestina Prima little else is known of his early life, and apart from assuming that he would have received a classical Greek Education the rest is deduction rather than based on known facts.

In 527, the first year of Eastern Roman Emperor Justinian I's reign, he became the adsessor (legal adviser) for Belisarius, Justinian's chief military commander who was then starting out on what would become a brilliant military career, initially in the East of the Empire.  After early successes Belisarius was defeated in 531 at the Battle of Callinicum and recalled to the Empire's heart in Constantinople.

Justinian was without doubt clever but cruel.  When part of Constantinople rose against him in the Nika riots of January, 532, he sent Belisarius and his fellow general Mundo to repress them in a savage massacre in the Hippodrome – witnessed by Procopius.

The following year Procopius accompanied Belisarius on his victorious expedition against the Vandal kingdom in North Africa and took part in the capture of Carthage.  Procopius remained in Northern Africa with Belisarius' successor, Solomon the Eunuch, when Belisarius returned to Constantinople.

Procopius rejoined Belisarius for his campaign against the Ostrogothic kingdom in Italy and was there for the Gothic siege of Rome that lasted a year and nine days and ended in March, 538. He witnessed Belisarius' entry into the Gothic capital, Ravenna, in 540.

However at some point in the next few years Procopius seems to have been moved away from working with Belisarius.  When the latter was sent back to Italy in 544 to cope with a further outbreak of the war with the Goths, Procopius appears to have no longer been with Belisarius' staff.

Procopius continued to record history and his works are both insightful and clear headed, distilling the complexities of the times into several classic books.

His death is thought to have been around 560.


## Index of Contents

Such, then, was the final outcome of the Persian War for the Emperor Justinian; and I shall now proceed to set forth all that he did against the Vandals and the Moors. But first shall be told whence came the host of the Vandals when they descended upon the land of the Romans. After Theodosius, the Roman Emperor, had departed from the world, having proved himself one of the most just of men and an able warrior, his kingdom was taken over by his two sons, Arcadius, the elder, receiving the Eastern portion, and Honorius, the younger, the Western. [Jan. 17, 395 A.D.] But the Roman power had been thus divided as far back as the time of Constantine and his sons; for he transferred his government to Byzantium, and making the city larger and much more renowned, allowed it to be named after him.

Now the earth is surrounded by a circle of ocean, either entirely or for the most part (for our knowledge is not as yet at all clear in this matter); and it is split into two continents by a sort of outflow from the ocean, a flow which enters at the western part and forms this Sea which we know, beginning at Gadira[1] and extending all the way to the Maeotic Lake.[2] Of these two continents the one to the right, as one sails into the Sea, as far as the Lake, has received the name of Asia, beginning at Gadira and at the southern[3] of the two Pillars of Heracles. Septem[4] is the name given by the natives to the fort at that point, since seven hills appear there; for "septem" has the force of "seven" in the Latin tongue. And the whole continent opposite this was named Europe. And the strait at that point separates the two continents[5] by about eighty-four stades, but from there on they are kept apart by wide expanses of sea as far as the Hellespont. For at this point they again approach each other at Sestus and Abydus, and once more at Byzantium and Chalcedon as far as the rocks called in ancient times the "Dark Blue Rocks," where even now is the place called Hieron. For at these places the continents are separated from one another by a distance of only ten stades and even less than that.

Now the distance from one of the Pillars of Heracles to the other, if one goes along the shore and does not pass around the Ionian Gulf and the sea called the Euxine but crosses from Chalcedon[6] to Byzantium and from Dryous[7] to the opposite mainland,[8] is a journey of two hundred and eighty-five days for an unencumbered traveller. For as to the land about the Euxine Sea, which extends from Byzantium to the Lake, it would be impossible to tell everything with precision, since the barbarians beyond the Ister River, which they also call the Danube, make the shore of that sea quite impossible for the Romans to traverse, except, indeed, that from Byzantium to the mouth of the Ister is a journey of twenty-two days, which should be added to the measure of Europe by one making the computation. And on the Asiatic side, that is from Chalcedon to the Phasis River, which, flowing from the country of the Colchians, descends into the Pontus, the journey is accomplished in forty days. So that the whole Roman domain, according to the distance along the sea at least, attains the measure of a three hundred and forty-seven days' journey, if, as has been said, one ferries over the Ionian Gulf, which extends about eight hundred stades from Dryous. For the passage across the gulf[9] amounts to a journey of not less than four days. Such, then, was the size of the Roman empire in the ancient times.

And there fell to him who held the power in the West the most of Libya, extending ninety days' journey, for such is the distance from Gadira to the boundaries of Tripolis in Libya; and in Europe he received as his portion territory extending seventy-five days' journey, for such is the distance from the northern[10] of the Pillars of Heracles to the Ionian Gulf.[11] And one might add also the distance around the gulf. And the emperor of the East received territory extending one hundred and twenty days' journey, from the boundaries of Cyrene in Libya as far as Epidamnus, which lies on the

Ionian Gulf and is called at the present time Dyrrachium, as well as that portion of the country about the Euxine Sea which, as previously stated, is subject to the Romans. Now one day's journey extends two hundred and ten stades,[12] or as far as from Athens to Megara. Thus, then, the Roman emperors divided either continent between them. And among the islands Britain, which is outside the Pillars of Heracles and by far the largest of all islands, was counted, as is natural, with the West; and inside the Pillars, Ebusa,[13] which lies in the Mediterranean in what we may call the Propontis, just inside the opening where the ocean enters, about seven days' journey from the opening, and two others near it, Majorica and Minorica, as they are called by the natives, were also assigned to the Western empire. And each of the islands in the Sea itself fell to the share of that one of the two emperors within whose boundaries it happened to lie.


II

Now while Honorius was holding the imperial power in the West, barbarians took possession of his land; and I shall tell who they were and in what manner they did so. [395-423 A.D.] There were many Gothic nations in earlier times, just as also at the present, but the greatest and most important of all are the Goths, Vandals, Visigoths, and Gepaedes. In ancient times, however, they were named Sauromatae and Melanchlaeni;[14] and there were some too who called these nations Getic. All these, while they are distinguished from one another by their names, as has been said, do not differ in anything else at all. For they all have white bodies and fair hair, and are tall and handsome to look upon, and they use the same laws and practise a common religion. For they are all of the Arian faith, and have one language called Gothic; and, as it seems to me, they all came originally from one tribe, and were distinguished later by the names of those who led each group. This people used to dwell above the Ister River from of old. Later on the Gepaedes got possession of the country about Singidunum[15] and Sirmium,[16] on both sides of the Ister River, where they have remained settled even down to my time.

But the Visigoths, separating from the others, removed from there and at first entered into an alliance with the Emperor Arcadius, but at a later time (for faith with the Romans cannot dwell in barbarians), under the leadership of Alaric, they became hostile to both emperors, and, beginning with Thrace, treated all Europe as an enemy's land. Now the Emperor Honorius had before this time been sitting in Rome, with never a thought of war in his mind, but glad, I think, if men allowed him to remain quiet in his palace. But when word was brought that the barbarians with a great army were not far off, but somewhere among the Taulantii,[17] he abandoned the palace and fled in disorderly fashion to Ravenna, a strong city lying just about at the end of the Ionian Gulf, while some say that he brought in the barbarians himself, because an uprising had been started against him among his subjects; but this does not seem to me trustworthy, as far, at least, as one can judge of the character of the man. And the barbarians, finding that they had no hostile force to encounter them, became the most cruel of all men. For they destroyed all the cities which they captured, especially those south of the Ionian Gulf, so completely that nothing has been left to my time to know them by, unless, indeed, it might be one tower or one gate or some such thing which chanced to remain. And they killed all the people, as many as came in their way, both old and young alike, sparing neither women nor children. Wherefore even up to the present time Italy is sparsely populated. They also gathered as plunder all the money out of all Europe, and, most important of all, they left in Rome nothing whatever of public or private wealth when they moved on to Gaul. But I shall now tell how Alaric captured Rome.

After much time had been spent by him in the siege, and he had not been able either by force or by any other device to capture the place, he formed the following plan. Among the youths in the army whose beards had not yet grown, but who had just come of age, he chose out three hundred whom he knew to be of good birth and possessed of valour beyond their years, and told them secretly that he was about to make a present of them to certain of the patricians in Rome, pretending that they were slaves. And he instructed them that, as soon as they got inside the houses of those men, they should display much gentleness and moderation and serve them eagerly in whatever tasks should be laid upon them by their owners; and he further directed them that not long afterwards, on an appointed day at about midday, when all those who were to be their masters would most likely be already asleep after their meal, they should all come to the gate called Salarian and with a sudden rush kill the guards, who would have no previous knowledge of the plot, and open the gates as quickly as possible. After giving these orders to the youths, Alaric straightway sent ambassadors to the members of the senate, stating that he admired them for their loyalty toward their emperor, and that he would trouble them no longer, because of their valour and faithfulness, with which it was plain that they were endowed to a remarkable degree, and in order that tokens of himself might be preserved among men both noble and brave, he wished to present each one of them with some domestics. After making this declaration and sending the youths not long afterwards, he commanded the barbarians to make preparations for the departure, and he let this be known to the Romans. And they heard his words gladly, and receiving the gifts began to be exceedingly happy, since they were completely ignorant of the plot of the barbarian. For the youths, by being unusually obedient to their owners, averted suspicion, and in the camp some were already seen moving from their positions and raising the siege, while it seemed that the others were just on the point of doing the very same thing. But when the appointed day had come, Alaric armed his whole force for the attack and was holding them in readiness close by the Salarian Gate; for it happened that he had encamped there at the beginning of the siege. And all the youths at the time of the day agreed upon came to this gate, and, assailing the guards suddenly, put them to death; then they opened the gates and received Alaric and the army into the city at their leisure. [Aug. 24, 410 A.D.] And they set fire to the houses which were next to the gate, among which was also the house of Sallust, who in ancient times wrote the history of the Romans, and the greater part of this house has stood half-burned up to my time; and after plundering the whole city and destroying the most of the Romans, they moved on. At that time they say that the Emperor Honorius in Ravenna received the message from one of the eunuchs, evidently a keeper of the poultry, that Rome had perished. And he cried out and said, "And yet it has just eaten from my hands!" For he had a very large cock, Rome by name; and the eunuch comprehending his words said that it was the city of Rome which had perished at the hands of Alaric, and the emperor with a sigh of relief answered quickly: "But I, my good fellow, thought that my fowl Rome had perished." So great, they say, was the folly with which this emperor was possessed.

But some say that Rome was not captured in this way by Alaric, but that Proba, a woman of very unusual eminence in wealth and in fame among the Roman senatorial class, felt pity for the Romans who were being destroyed by hunger and the other suffering they endured; for they were already even tasting each other's flesh; and seeing that every good hope had left them, since both the river and the harbour were held by the enemy, she commanded her domestics, they say, to open the gates by night.

Now when Alaric was about to depart from Rome, he declared Attalus, one of their nobles, emperor of the Romans, investing him with the diadem and the purple and whatever else pertains to the imperial dignity. And he did this with the intention of removing Honorius from his throne and of giving over the whole power in the West to Attalus. With such a purpose, then, both Attalus and Alaric were going with a great army against Ravenna. But this Attalus was neither able to think wisely himself, nor to be persuaded by one who had wisdom to offer. So while Alaric did not by any means approve the plan, Attalus sent commanders to Libya without an army. Thus, then, were these things going on.

And the island of Britain revolted from the Romans, and the soldiers there chose as their king Constantinus, a man of no mean station. [407 A.D.] And he straightway gathered a fleet of ships and a formidable army and invaded both Spain and Gaul with a great force, thinking to enslave these countries. But Honorius was holding ships in readiness and waiting to see what would happen in Libya, in order that, if those sent by Attalus were repulsed, he might himself sail for Libya and keep some portion of his own kingdom, while if matters there should go against him, he might reach Theodosius and remain with him. For Arcadius had already died long before, and his son Theodosius, still a very young child,[18] held the power of the East. [408-450 A.D.] But while Honorius was thus anxiously awaiting the outcome of these events and tossed amid the billows of uncertain fortune, it so chanced that some wonderful pieces of good fortune befell him. For God is accustomed to succour those who are neither clever nor able to devise anything of themselves, and to lend them assistance, if they be not wicked, when they are in the last extremity of despair; such a thing, indeed, befell this emperor. For it was suddenly reported from Libya that the commanders of Attalus had been destroyed, and that a host of ships was at hand from Byzantium with a very great number of soldiers who had come to assist him, though he had not expected them, and that Alaric, having quarrelled with Attalus, had stripped him of the emperor's garb and was now keeping him under guard in the position of a private citizen. [411 A.D.] And afterwards Alaric died of disease, and the army of the Visigoths under the leadership of Adaulphus proceeded into Gaul, and Constantinus, defeated in battle, died with his sons. However the Romans never succeeded in recovering Britain, but it remained from that time on under tyrants. And the Goths, after making the crossing of the Ister, at first occupied Pannonia, but afterwards, since the emperor gave them the right, they inhabited the country of Thrace. And after spending no great time there they conquered the West. But this will be told in the narrative concerning the Goths.


III


Now the Vandals dwelling about the Maeotic Lake, since they were pressed by hunger, moved to the country of the Germans, who are now called Franks, and the river Rhine, associating with themselves the Alani, a Gothic people. Then from there, under the leadership of Godigisclus, they moved and settled in Spain, which is the first land of the Roman empire on the side of the ocean. At that time Honorius made an agreement with Godigisclus that they should settle there on condition that it should not be to the detriment of the country. But there was a law among the Romans, that if any persons should fail to keep their property in their own possession, and if, meanwhile, a time amounting to thirty years should pass, that these persons should thenceforth not be entitled to proceed against those who had forced them out, but they were excluded by demurrer[19] from access to the court; and in view of this he established a law that whatever time should be spent by the Vandals in the Roman domain should not by any means be counted toward this thirty-year demurrer. And Honorius himself, when the West had been driven by him to this pass, died of disease. [Aug. 27, 423 A.D.] Now before this, as it happened, the royal power had been shared by Honorius with Constantius, the husband of Placidia, the sister of Arcadius and Honorius; but he lived to exercise the power only a few days, and then, becoming seriously ill, he died while Honorius was still living, [421 A.D.] having never succeeded in saying or in doing anything worth recounting; for the time was not sufficient during which he lived in possession of the royal power. Now a son of this Constantius, Valentinian, a child just weaned, was being reared in the palace of Theodosius, but the members of the imperial court in Rome chose one of the soldiers there, John by name, as emperor. This man was both gentle and well-endowed with sagacity and thoroughly capable of valorous deeds. At any rate he held the tyranny five years[20] and directed it with moderation, and he neither gave ear to slanderers nor did he do any unjust murder, willingly at least, nor did he set his hand to robbing men of money; but he did not prove able to do anything at all against the barbarians, since his relations with Byzantium were hostile. Against this John, Theodosius, the son of Arcadius, sent a great army and Aspar and Ardaburius, the son of Aspar, as generals, and wrested from him the tyranny and gave over the royal power to Valentinian, who was still a child. And Valentinian took John alive, and he brought him out in the hippodrome of Aquileia with one of his hands cut off and caused him to ride in state on an ass, and then after he had suffered much ill treatment from the stage-performers there, both in word and in deed, he put him to death. [426 A.D.] Thus Valentinian took over the power of the West. But Placidia, his mother, had reared this emperor and educated him in an altogether effeminate manner, and in consequence he was filled with wickedness from childhood. For he associated mostly with sorcerers and those who busy themselves with the stars, and, being an extraordinarily zealous pursuer of love affairs with other men's wives, he conducted himself in a most indecent manner, although he was married to a woman of exceptional beauty. [455 A.D.] And not only was this true, but he also failed to recover for the empire anything of what had been wrested from it before, and he both lost Libya in addition to the territory previously lost and was himself destroyed. And when he perished, it fell to the lot of his wife and his children to become captives. Now the disaster in Libya came about as follows.

There were two Roman generals, Aetius and Boniface, especially valiant men and in experience of many wars inferior to none of that time at least. These two came to be at variance in regard to matters of state, but they attained to such a degree of highmindedness and excellence in every respect that if one should call either of them "the last of the Romans" he would not err, so true was it that all the excellent qualities of the Romans were summed up in these two men. One of these, Boniface, was appointed by Placidia general of all Libya. Now this was not in accord with the wishes of Aetius, but he by no means disclosed the fact that it did not please him. For their hostility had not as yet come to light, but was concealed behind the countenance of each. But when Boniface had got out of the way, Aetius slandered him to Placidia, saying that he was setting up a tyranny and had robbed her and the emperor of all Libya, and he said that it was very easy for her to find out the truth; for if she should summon Boniface to Rome, he would never come. And when the woman heard this, Aetius seemed to her to speak well and she acted accordingly. But Aetius, anticipating her, wrote to Boniface secretly that the mother of the emperor was plotting against him and wished to put him out of the way. And he predicted to him that there would be convincing proof of the plot; for he would be summoned very shortly for no reason at all. Such was the announcement of the letter. And Boniface did not disregard the message, for as soon as those arrived who were summoning him to the emperor, he refused to give heed to the emperor and his mother, disclosing to no one the warning of Aetius. So when Placidia heard this, she thought that Aetius was exceedingly well-disposed towards the emperor's cause and took under consideration the question of Boniface. But Boniface, since it did not seem to him that he was able to array himself against the emperor, and since if he returned to Rome there was clearly no safety for him, began to lay plans so that, if possible, he might have a defensive alliance with the Vandals, who, as previously stated, had established themselves in Spain not far from Libya. There Godigisclus had died and the royal power had fallen to his sons, Gontharis, who was born to him from his wedded wife, and Gizeric,[21] of illegitimate birth. But the former was still a child and not of very energetic temper, while Gizeric had been excellently trained in warfare, and was the cleverest of all men. Boniface accordingly sent to Spain those who were his own most intimate friends and gained the adherence of each of the sons of Godigisclus on terms of complete equality, it being agreed that each one of the three, holding a third part of Libya, should rule over his own subjects; but if a foe should come against any one of them to make war, that they should in common ward off the aggressors. On the basis of this agreement the Vandals crossed the strait at Gadira and came into Libya, and the Visigoths in later times settled in Spain. But in Rome the friends of Boniface, remembering the character of the man and considering how strange his action was, were greatly astonished to think that Boniface was setting up a tyranny, and some of them at the order of Placidia went to Carthage. There they met Boniface, and saw the letter of Aetius, and after hearing the whole story they returned to Rome as quickly as they could and reported to Placidia how Boniface stood in relation to her. And though the woman was dumbfounded, she did nothing unpleasant to Aetius nor did she upbraid him for what he had done to the emperor's house, for he himself wielded great power and the affairs of the empire were already in an evil plight; but she disclosed to the friends of Boniface the advice Aetius had given, and, offering oaths and pledges of safety, entreated them to persuade the man, if they could, to return to his fatherland and not to permit the empire of the Romans to lie under the hand of barbarians. And when Boniface heard this, he repented of his act and of his agreement with the barbarians, and he besought them incessantly, promising them everything, to remove from Libya. But since they did not receive his words with favour, but considered that they were being insulted, he was compelled to fight with them, and being defeated in the battle, he retired to Hippo[22] Regius, a strong city in the portion of Numidia that is on the sea. There the Vandals made camp under the leadership of Gizeric and began a siege; for Gontharis had already died. And they say that he perished at the hand of his brother. The Vandals, however, do not agree with those who make this statement, but say that Gontharis' was captured in battle by Germans in Spain and impaled, and that Gizeric was already sole ruler when he led the Vandals into Libya. This, indeed, I have heard from the Vandals, stated in this way. But after much time had passed by, since they were unable to secure Hippo Regius either by force or by surrender, and since at the same time they were being pressed by hunger, they raised the siege. And a little later Boniface and the Romans in Libya, since a numerous army had come from both Rome and Byzantium and Aspar with them as general, decided to renew the struggle, and a fierce battle was fought in which they were badly beaten by the enemy, and they made haste to flee as each one could. And Aspar betook himself homeward, and Boniface, coming before Placidia, acquitted himself of the suspicion, showing that it had arisen against him for no true cause.


IV

So the Vandals, having wrested Libya from the Romans in this way, made it their own. And those of the enemy whom they took alive they reduced to slavery and held under guard. Among these happened to be Marcian, who later upon the death of Theodosius assumed the imperial power. At that time, however, Gizeric commanded that the captives be brought into the king's courtyard, in order that it might be possible for him, by looking at them, to know what master each of them might serve without degradation. And when they were gathered under the open sky, about midday, the season being summer, they were distressed by the sun and sat down. And somewhere or other among them Marcian, quite neglected, was sleeping. Then an eagle flew over him spreading out his wings, as they say, and always remaining in the same place in the air he cast a shadow over Marcian alone. And Gizeric, upon seeing from the upper storey what was happening, since he was an exceedingly discerning person, suspected that the thing was a divine manifestation, and summoning the man enquired of him who he might be. And he replied that he was a confidential adviser of Aspar; such a person the Romans call a "domesticus" in their own tongue. And when Gizeric heard this and considered first the meaning of the bird's action, and then remembered how great power Aspar exercised in Byzantium, it became evident to him that the man was being led to royal power. He therefore by no means deemed it right to kill him, reasoning that, if he should remove him from the world, it would be very clear that the thing which the bird had done was nothing (for he would not honour with his shadow a king who was about to die straightway), and he felt, too, that he would be killing him for no good cause; and if, on the other hand, it was fated that in later times the man should become king, it would never be within his power to inflict death upon him; for that which has been decided upon by God could never be prevented by a man's decision. But he bound Marcian by oaths that, if it should be in his power, he would never take up arms against the Vandals at least. [450 A.D.] Thus, then, Marcian was released and came to Byzantium, and when at a later time Theodosius died he received the empire. And in all other respects he proved himself a good emperor, but he paid no attention at all to affairs in Libya. But this happened in later times.

At that time Gizeric, after conquering Aspar and Boniface in battle, displayed a foresight worth recounting, whereby he made his good fortune most thoroughly secure. For fearing lest, if once again an army should come against him from both Rome and Byzantium, the Vandals might not be able to use the same strength and enjoy the same fortune, (since human affairs are wont to be overturned by Heaven and to fail by reason of the weakness of men's bodies), he was not lifted up by the good fortune he had enjoyed, but rather became moderate because of what he feared, and so he made a treaty with the Emperor Valentinian providing that each year he should pay to the emperor tribute from Libya, and he delivered over one of his sons, Honoric, as a hostage to make this agreement binding. So Gizeric both showed himself a brave man in the battle and guarded the victory as securely as possible, and, since the friendship between the two peoples increased greatly, he received back his son Honoric. And at Rome Placidia had died before this time, and after her, Valentinian, her son, also died, having no male offspring, but two daughters had been born to him from Eudoxia, the child of Theodosius. And I shall now relate in what manner Valentinian died.

There was a certain Maximus, a Roman senator, of the house of that Maximus[23] who, while usurping the imperial power, was overthrown by the elder Theodosius and put to death, and on whose account also the Romans celebrate the annual festival named from the defeat of Maximus. This younger Maximus was married to a woman discreet in her ways and exceedingly famous for her beauty. For this reason a desire came over Valentinian to have her to wife. And since it was impossible, much as he wished it, to meet her, he plotted an unholy deed and carried it to fulfilment. For he summoned Maximus to the palace and sat down with him to a game of draughts, and a certain sum was set as a penalty for the loser; and the emperor won in this game, and receiving Maximus' ring as a pledge for the agreed amount, he sent it to his house, instructing the messenger to tell the wife of Maximus that her husband bade her come as quickly as possible to the palace to salute the queen Eudoxia. And she, judging by the ring that the message was from Maximus, entered her litter and was conveyed to the emperor's court. And she was received by those who had been assigned this service by the emperor, and led into a certain room far removed from the women's apartments, where Valentinian met her and forced her, much against her will. And she, after the outrage, went to her husband's house weeping and feeling the deepest possible grief because of her misfortune, and she cast many curses upon Maximus as having provided the cause for what had been done. Maximus, accordingly, became exceedingly aggrieved at that which had come to pass, and straightway entered into a conspiracy against the emperor; but when he saw that Aetius was exceedingly powerful, for he had recently conquered Attila, who had invaded the Roman domain with a great army of Massagetae and the other Scythians, the thought occurred to him that Aetius would be in the way of his undertaking. And upon considering this matter, it seemed to him that it was the better course to put Aetius out of the way first, paying no heed to the fact that the whole hope of the Romans centred in him. And since the eunuchs who were in attendance upon the emperor were well-disposed toward him, he persuaded the emperor by their devices that Aetius was setting on foot a revolution. And Valentinian, judging by nothing else than the power and valour of Aetius that the report was true, put the man to death. [Sept. 21, 454 A.D.] Whereupon a certain Roman made himself famous by a saying which he uttered. For when the emperor enquired of him whether he had done well in putting Aetius to death, he replied saying that, as to this matter, he was not able to know whether he had done well or perhaps otherwise, but one thing he understood exceedingly well, that he had cut off his own right hand with the other.

So after the death of Aetius,[24] Attila, since no one was a match for him, plundered all Europe with no trouble and made both emperors subservient and tributary to himself. For tribute money was sent to him every year by the emperors. At that time, while Attila was besieging Aquileia, a city of great size and exceedingly populous situated near the sea and above the Ionian Gulf, they say that the following good fortune befell him. For they tell the story that, when he was able to capture the place neither by force nor by any other means, he gave up the siege in despair, since it had already lasted a long time, and commanded the whole army without any delay to make their preparations for the departure, in order that on the morrow all might move from there at sunrise. And the following day about sunrise, the barbarians had raised the siege and were already beginning the departure, when a single male stork which had a nest on a certain tower of the city wall and was rearing his nestlings there suddenly rose and left the place with his young. And the father stork was flying, but the little storks, since they were not yet quite ready to fly, were at times sharing their father's flight and at times riding upon his back, and thus they flew off and went far away from the city. And when Attila saw this (for he was most clever at comprehending and interpreting all things), he commanded the army, they say, to remain still in the same place, adding that the bird would never have gone flying off at random from there with his nestlings, unless he was prophesying that some evil would come to the place at no distant time. Thus, they say, the army of the barbarians settled down to the siege once more, and not long after that a portion of the wall, the very part which held the nest of that bird, for no apparent reason suddenly fell down, and it became possible for the enemy to enter the city at that point, and thus Aquileia was captured by storm. Such is the story touching Aquileia.

Later on Maximus slew the emperor with no trouble and secured the tyranny, and he married Eudoxia by force. [455 A.D.] For the wife to whom he had been wedded had died not long before. And on one occasion in private he made the statement to Eudoxia that it was all for the sake of her love that he had carried out all that he had done. And since she felt a repulsion for Maximus even before that time, and had been desirous of exacting vengeance from him for the wrong done Valentinian, his words made her swell with rage still more against him, and led her on to carry out her plot, since she had heard Maximus say that on account of her the misfortune had befallen her husband. And as soon as day came, she sent to Carthage entreating Gizeric to avenge Valentinian, who had been destroyed by an unholy man, in a manner unworthy both of himself and of his imperial station, and to deliver her, since she was suffering unholy treatment at the hand of the tyrant. And she impressed it upon Gizeric that, since he was a friend and ally and so great a calamity had befallen the imperial house, it was not a holy thing to fail to become an avenger. For from Byzantium she thought no vengeance would come, since Theodosius had already departed from the world and Marcian had taken over the empire. [Mar. 17, 455 A.D.]

V

And Gizeric, for no other reason than that he suspected that much money would come to him, set sail for Italy with a great fleet. And going up to Rome, since no one stood in his way, he took possession of the palace. Now while Maximus was trying to flee, the Romans threw stones at him and killed him, and they cut off his head and each of his other members and divided them among themselves. But Gizeric took Eudoxia captive, together with Eudocia and Placidia, the children of herself and Valentinian, and placing an exceedingly great amount of gold and other imperial treasure[25] in his ships sailed to Carthage, having spared neither bronze nor anything else whatsoever in the palace. He plundered also the temple of Jupiter Capitolinus, and tore off half of the roof. Now this roof was of bronze of the finest quality, and since gold was laid over it exceedingly thick, it shone as a magnificent and wonderful spectacle.[26] But of the ships with Gizeric, one, which was bearing the statues, was lost, they say, but with all the others the Vandals reached port in the harbour of Carthage. Gizeric then married Eudocia to Honoric, the elder of his sons; but the other of the two women, being the wife of Olybrius, a most distinguished man in the Roman senate, he sent to Byzantium together with her mother, Eudoxia, at the request of the emperor. Now the power of the East had by now fallen to Leon, who had been set in this position by Aspar, since Marcian had already passed from the world. [457 A.D.]

Afterwards Gizeric devised the following scheme. He tore down the walls of all the cities in Libya except Carthage, so that neither the Libyans themselves, espousing the cause of the Romans, might have a strong base from which to begin a rebellion, nor those sent by the emperor have any ground for hoping to capture a city and by establishing a garrison in it to make trouble for the Vandals. Now at that time it seemed that he had counselled well and had ensured prosperity for the Vandals in the safest possible manner; but in later times when these cities, being without walls, were captured by Belisarius all the more easily and with less exertion, Gizeric was then condemned to suffer much ridicule, and that which for the time he considered wise counsel turned out for him to be folly. For as fortunes change, men are always accustomed to change with them their judgments regarding what has been planned in the past. And among the Libyans all who happened to be men of note and conspicuous for their wealth he handed over as slaves, together with their estates and all their money, to his sons Honoric and Genzon. For Theodorus, the youngest son, had died already, being altogether without offspring, either male or female. And he robbed the rest of the Libyans of their estates, which were both very numerous and excellent, and distributed them among the nation of the Vandals, and as a result of this these lands have been called "Vandals' estates" up to the present time. And it fell to the lot of those who had formerly possessed these lands to be in extreme poverty and to be at the same time free men; and they had the privilege of going away wheresoever they wished. And Gizeric commanded that all the lands which he had given over to his sons and to the other Vandals should not be subject to any kind of taxation. But as much of the land as did not seem to him good he allowed to remain in the hands of the former owners, but assessed so large a sum to be paid on this land for taxes to the government that nothing whatever remained to those who retained their farms. And many of them were constantly being sent into exile or killed. For charges were brought against them of many sorts, and heavy ones too; but one charge seemed to be the greatest of all, that a man, having money of his own, was hiding it. Thus the Libyans were visited with every form of misfortune.

The Vandals and the Alani he arranged in companies, appointing over them no less than eighty captains, whom he called "chiliarchs,"[27] making it appear that his host of fighting men in active service amounted to eighty thousand. And yet the number of the Vandals and Alani was said in former times, at least, to amount to no more than fifty thousand men. However, after that time by their natural increase among themselves and by associating other barbarians with them they came to be an exceedingly numerous people. But the names of the Alani and all the other barbarians, except the Moors, were united in the name of Vandals. At that time, after the death of Valentinian, Gizeric gained the support of the Moors, and every year at the beginning of spring he made invasions into Sicily and Italy, enslaving some of the cities, razing others to the ground, and plundering everything; and when the land had become destitute of men and of money, he invaded the domain of the emperor of the East. And so he plundered Illyricum and the most of the Peloponnesus and of the rest of Greece and all the islands which lie near it. And again he went off to Sicily and Italy, and kept plundering and pillaging all places in turn. And one day when he had embarked on his ship in the harbour of Carthage, and the sails were already being spread, the pilot asked him, they say, against what men in the world he bade them go. And he in reply said: "Plainly against those with whom God is angry." Thus without any cause he kept making invasions wherever chance might lead him.


VI


And the Emperor Leon, wishing to punish the Vandals because of these things, was gathering an army against them; and they say that this army amounted to about one hundred thousand men. And he collected a fleet of ships from the whole of the eastern Mediterranean, shewing great generosity to both soldiers and sailors, for he feared lest from a parsimonious policy some obstacle might arise to hinder him in his desire to carry out his punishment of the barbarians. Therefore, they say, thirteen hundred centenaria[28] were expended by him to no purpose. But since it was not fated that the Vandals should be destroyed by this expedition, he made Basiliscus commander-in-chief, the brother of his wife Berine, a man who was extraordinarily desirous of the royal power, which he hoped would come to him without a struggle if he won the friendship of Aspar. For Aspar himself, being an adherent of the Arian faith, and having no intention of changing it for another, was unable to enter upon the imperial office, but he was easily strong enough to establish another in it, and it already seemed likely that he would plot against the Emperor Leon, who had given him offence. So they say that since Aspar was then fearful lest, if the Vandals were defeated, Leon should establish his power most securely, he repeatedly urged upon Basiliscus that he should spare the Vandals and Gizeric.

[467 A.D.] Now before this time Leon had already appointed and sent Anthemius, as Emperor of the West, a man of the senate of great wealth and high birth, in order that he might assist him in the Vandalic war. And yet Gizeric kept asking and earnestly entreating that the imperial power be given to Olybrius, who was married to Placidia, the daughter of Valentinian, and on account of his relationship[29] well-disposed toward him, and when he failed in this he was still more angry and kept plundering the whole land of the emperor. Now there was in Dalmatia a certain Marcellianus, one of the acquaintances of Aetius and a man of repute, who, after Aetius had died in the manner told above,[30] no longer deigned to yield obedience to the emperor, but beginning a revolution and detaching all the others from allegiance, held the power of Dalmatia himself, since no one dared encounter him. But the Emperor Leon at that time won over this Marcellianus by very careful wheedling, and bade him go to the island of Sardinia, which was then subject to the Vandals. And he drove out the Vandals and gained possession of it with no great difficulty. And Heracleius was sent from Byzantium to Tripolis in Libya, and after conquering the Vandals of that district in battle, he easily captured the cities, and leaving his ships there, led his army on foot toward Carthage. Such, then, was the sequence of events which formed the prelude of the war.

But Basiliscus with his whole fleet put in at a town distant from Carthage no less than two hundred and eighty stades (now it so happened that a temple of Hermes had been there from of old, from which fact the place was named Mercurium; for the Romans call Hermes "Mercurius"), and if he had not purposely played the coward and hesitated, but had undertaken to go straight for Carthage, he would have captured it at the first onset, and he would have reduced the Vandals to subjection without their even thinking of resistance; so overcome was Gizeric with awe of Leon as an invincible emperor, when the report was brought to him that Sardinia and Tripolis had been captured, and he saw the fleet of Basiliscus to be such as the Romans were said never to have had before. But, as it was, the general's hesitation, whether caused by cowardice or treachery, prevented this success. And Gizeric, profiting by the negligence of Basiliscus, did as follows. Arming all his subjects in the best way he could, he filled his ships, but not all, for some he kept in readiness empty, and they were the ships which sailed most swiftly. And sending envoys to Basiliscus, he begged him to defer the war for the space of five days, in order that in the meantime he might take counsel and do those things which were especially desired by the emperor. They say, too, that he sent also a great amount of gold without the knowledge of the army of Basiliscus and thus purchased this armistice. And he did this, thinking, as actually did happen, that a favouring wind would rise for him during this time. And Basiliscus, either as doing a favour to Aspar in accordance with what he had promised, or selling the moment of opportunity for money, or perhaps thinking it the better course, did as he was requested and remained quietly in the camp, awaiting the moment favourable to the enemy.

But the Vandals, as soon as the wind had arisen for them which they had been expecting during the time they lay at rest, raised their sails and, taking in tow the boats which, as has been stated above, they had made ready with no men in them, they sailed against the enemy. And when they came near, they set fire to the boats which they were towing, when their sails were bellied by the wind, and let them go against the Roman fleet. And since there were a great number of ships there, these boats easily spread fire wherever they struck, and were themselves readily destroyed together with those with which they came in contact. And as the fire advanced in this way the Roman fleet was filled with tumult, as was natural, and with a great din that rivalled the noise caused by the wind and the roaring of the flames, as the soldiers together with the sailors shouted orders to one another and pushed off with their poles the fire-boats and their own ships as well, which were being destroyed by one another in complete disorder. And already the Vandals too were at hand ramming and sinking the ships, and making booty of such of the soldiers as attempted to escape, and of their arms as well. But there were also some of the Romans who proved themselves brave men in this struggle, and most of all John, who was a general under Basiliscus and who had no share whatever in his treason. For a great throng having surrounded his ship, he stood on the deck, and turning from side to side kept killing very great numbers of the enemy from there, and when he perceived that the ship was being captured, he leaped with his whole equipment of arms from the deck into the sea. And though Genzon, the son of Gizeric, entreated him earnestly not to do this, offering pledges and holding out promises of safety, he nevertheless threw himself into the sea, uttering this one word, that John would never come under the hands of dogs.

So this war came to an end, and Heracleius departed for home; for Marcellianus had been destroyed treacherously by one of his fellow-officers. And Basiliscus, coming to Byzantium, seated himself as a suppliant in the sanctuary of Christ the Great God ("Sophia"[31] the temple is called by the men of Byzantium who consider that this designation is especially appropriate to God), and although, by the intercession of Berine, the queen, he escaped this danger, he was not able at that time to reach the throne, the thing for the sake of which everything had been done by him. For the Emperor Leon not long afterwards destroyed both Aspar and Ardaburius in the palace, because he suspected that they were plotting against his life. [471 A.D.] Thus, then, did these events take place.


VII

[Aug. 11, 472 A.D.] Now Anthemius, the emperor of the West, died at the hand of his son-in-law Rhecimer, and Olybrius, succeeding to the throne, a short time afterward suffered the same fate. [Oct. 10, 472 A.D.] And when Leon also had died in Byzantium, the imperial office was taken over by the younger Leon, the son of Zeno and Ariadne, the daughter of Leon, while he was still only a few days old. And his father having been chosen as partner in the royal power, the child forthwith passed from the world. [474 A.D.] Majorinus also deserves mention, who had gained the power of the West before this time. For this Majorinus, who surpassed in every virtue all who have ever been emperors of the Romans, did not bear lightly the loss of Libya, but collected a very considerable army against the Vandals and came to Liguria, intending himself to lead the army against the enemy. For Majorinus never showed the least hesitation before any task and least of all before the dangers of war. But thinking it not inexpedient for him to investigate first the strength of the Vandals and the character of Gizeric and to discover how the Moors and Libyans stood with regard to friendship or hostility toward the Romans, he decided to trust no eyes other than his own in such a matter. Accordingly he set out as if an envoy from the emperor to Gizeric, assuming some fictitious name. And fearing lest, by becoming known, he should himself receive some harm and at the same time prevent the success of the enterprise, he devised the following scheme. His hair, which was famous among all men as being so fair as to resemble pure gold, he anointed with some kind of dye, which was especially invented for this purpose, and so succeeded completely in changing it for the time to a dark hue. And when he came before Gizeric, the barbarian attempted in many ways to terrify him, and in particular, while treating him with engaging attention, as if a friend, he brought him into the house where all his weapons were stored, a numerous and exceedingly noteworthy array. Thereupon they say that the weapons shook of their own accord and gave forth a sound of no ordinary or casual sort, and then it seemed to Gizeric that there had been an earthquake, but when he got outside and made enquiries concerning the earthquake, since no one else agreed with him, a great wonder, they say, came over him, but he was not able to comprehend the meaning of what had happened. So Majorinus, having accomplished the very things he wished, returned to Liguria, and leading his army on foot, came to the Pillars of Heracles, purposing to cross over the strait at that point, and then to march by land from there against Carthage. And when Gizeric became aware of this, and perceived that he had been tricked by Majorinus in the matter of the embassy, he became alarmed and made his preparations for war. And the Romans, basing their confidence on the valour of Majorinus, already began to have fair hopes of recovering Libya for the empire. [461 A.D.] But meantime Majorinus was attacked by the disease of dysentery and died, a man who had shewn himself moderate toward his subjects, and an object of fear to his enemies. [July 24, 474 A.D.] And another emperor, Nepos, upon taking over the empire, and living to enjoy it only a few days, died of disease, and Glycerius after him entered into this office and suffered a similar fate. [474-475 A.D.] And after him Augustus assumed the imperial power. There were, moreover, still other emperors in the West before this time, but though I know their names well, I shall make no mention of them whatever. For it so fell out that they lived only a short time after attaining the office, and as a result of this accomplished nothing worthy of mention. Such was the course of events in the West.

But in Byzantium Basiliscus, being no longer able to master his passion for royal power, made an attempt to usurp the throne, and succeeded without difficulty, since Zeno, together with his wife, sought refuge in Isauria, which was his native home. [471 A.D.] And while he was maintaining his tyranny for a year and eight months he was detested by practically everyone and in particular by the soldiers of the court on account of the greatness of his avarice. And Zeno, perceiving this, collected an army and came against him. And Basiliscus sent an army under the general Harmatus in order to array himself against Zeno. But when they had made camp near one another, Harmatus surrendered his army to Zeno, on the condition that Zeno should appoint as Caesar Harmatus' son Basiliscus, who was a very young child, and leave him as successor to the throne upon his death. And Basiliscus, deserted by all, fled for refuge to the same sanctuary as formerly. And Acacius, the priest of the city, put him into the hands of Zeno, charging him with impiety and with having brought great confusion and many innovations into the Christian doctrine, having inclined toward the heresy of Eutyches. And this was so. And after Zeno had thus taken over the empire a second time, he carried out his pledge to Harmatus formally by appointing his son Basiliscus Caesar, but not long afterwards he both stripped him of the office and put Harmatus to death. And he sent Basiliscus together with his children and his wife into Cappadocia in the winter season, commanding that they should be destitute of food and clothes and every kind of care. And there, being hard pressed by both cold and hunger, they took refuge in one another's arms, and embracing their loved ones, perished. And this punishment overtook Basiliscus for the policy he had pursued. These things, however, happened in later times.

But at that time Gizeric was plundering the whole Roman domain just as much as before, if not more, circumventing his enemy by craft and driving them out of their possessions by force, as has been previously said, and he continued to do so until the emperor Zeno came to an agreement with him and an endless peace was established between them, by which it was provided that the Vandals should never in all time perform any hostile act against the Romans nor suffer such a thing at their hands. And this peace was preserved by Zeno himself and also by his successor in the empire, Anastasius And it remained in force until the time of the emperor Justinus. But Justinian, who was the nephew of Justinus, succeeded him in the imperial power, and it was in the reign of this Justinian that the war with which we are concerned came to pass, in the manner which will be told in the following narrative. [477 A.D.] Gizeric, after living on a short time, died at an advanced age, having made a will in which he enjoined many things upon the Vandals and in particular that the royal power among them should always fall to that one who should be the first in years among all the male offspring descended from Gizeric himself. So Gizeric, having ruled over the Vandals thirty-nine years from the time when he captured Carthage, died, as I have said.

VIII

And Honoric, the eldest of his sons, succeeded to the throne, Genzon having already departed from the world. During the time when this Honoric ruled the Vandals they had no war against anyone at all, except the Moors. For through fear of Gizeric the Moors had remained quiet before that time, but as soon as he was out of their way they both did much harm to the Vandals and suffered the same themselves. And Honoric shewed himself the most cruel and unjust of all men toward the Christians in Libya. For he forced them to change over to the Arian faith, and as many as he found not readily yielding to him he burned, or destroyed by other forms of death; and he also cut off the tongues of many from the very throat, who even up to my time were going about in Byzantium having their speech uninjured, and perceiving not the least effect from this punishment; but two of these, since they saw fit to go in to harlots, were thenceforth no longer able to speak. And after ruling over the Vandals eight years he died of disease; and by that time the Moors dwelling on Mt. Aurasium[32] had revolted from the Vandals and were independent (this Aurasium is a mountain of Numidia, about thirteen days' journey distant from Carthage and fronting the south); and indeed they never came under the Vandals again, since the latter were unable to carry on a war against Moors on a mountain difficult of access and exceedingly steep.

After the death of Honoric the rule of the Vandals fell to Gundamundus, the son of Genzon, the son of Gizeric. [485 A.D.] For he, in point of years, was the first of the offspring of Gizeric. This Gundamundus fought against the Moors in numerous encounters, and after subjecting the Christians to still greater suffering, he died of disease, being now at about the middle of the twelfth year of his reign. [496 A.D.] And his brother Trasamundus took over the kingdom, a man well-favoured in appearance and especially gifted with discretion and highmindedness. However he continued to force the Christians to change their ancestral faith, not by torturing their bodies as his predecessors had done, but by seeking to win them with honours and offices and presenting them with great sums of money; and in the case of those who would not be persuaded, he pretended he had not the least knowledge of what manner of men they were.[33] And if he caught any guilty of great crimes which they had committed either by accident or deliberate intent, he would offer such men, as a reward for changing their faith, that they should not be punished for their offences. And when his wife died without becoming the mother of either male or female offspring, wishing to establish the kingdom as securely as possible, he sent to Theoderic, the king of the Goths, asking him to give him his sister Amalafrida to wife, for her husband had just died. And Theoderic sent him not only his sister but also a thousand of the notable Goths as a bodyguard, who were followed by a host of attendants amounting to about five thousand fighting men. And Theoderic also presented his sister with one of the promontories of Sicily, which are three in number, the one which they call Lilybaeum, and as a result of this Trasamundus was accounted the strongest and most powerful of all those who had ruled over the Vandals. He became also a very special friend of the emperor Anastasius. It was during the reign of Trasamundus that it came about that the Vandals suffered a disaster at the hands of the Moors such as had never befallen them before that time.

There was a certain Cabaon ruling over the Moors of Tripolis, a man experienced in many wars and exceedingly shrewd. This Cabaon, upon learning that the Vandals were marching against him, did as follows. First of all he issued orders to his subjects to abstain from all injustice and from all foods tending towards luxury and most of all from association with women; and setting up two palisaded enclosures, he encamped himself with all the men in one, and in the other he shut the women, and he threatened that death would be the penalty if anyone should go to the women's palisade. And after this he sent spies to Carthage with the following instructions: whenever the Vandals in going forth on the expedition should offer insult to any temple which the Christians reverence, they were to look on and see what took place; and when the Vandals had passed the place, they were to do the opposite of everything which the Vandals had done to the sanctuary before their departure. And they say that he added this also, that he was ignorant of the God whom the Christians worshipped, but it was probable that if He was powerful, as He was said to be, He should wreak vengeance upon those who insulted Him and defend those who honoured Him. So the spies came to Carthage and waited quietly, observing the preparation of the Vandals; but when the army set out on the march to Tripolis, they followed, clothing themselves in humble garb. And the Vandals, upon making camp the first day, led their horses and their other animals into the temples of the Christians, and sparing no insult, they acted with all the unrestrained lawlessness natural to them, beating as many priests as they caught and lashing them with many blows over the back and commanding them to render such service to the Vandals as they were accustomed to assign to the most dishonoured of their domestics. And as soon as they had departed from there, the spies of Cabaon did as they had been directed to do; for they straightway cleansed the sanctuaries and took away with great care the filth and whatever other unholy thing lay in them, and they lighted all the lamps and bowed down before the priests with great reverence and saluted them with all friendliness; and after giving pieces of silver to the poor who sat about these sanctuaries, they then followed after the army of the Vandals. And from then on along the whole route the Vandals continued to commit the same offences and the spies to render the same service. And when they were coming near the Moors, the spies anticipated them and reported to Cabaon what had been done by the Vandals and by themselves to the temples of the Christians, and that the enemy were somewhere near by. And Cabaon, upon learning this, arranged for the encounter as follows. He marked off a circle in the plain where he was about to make his palisade, and placed his camels turned sideways in a circle as a protection for the camp, making his line fronting the enemy about twelve camels deep. Then he placed the children and the women and all those who were unfit for fighting together with their possessions in the middle, while he commanded the host of fighting men to stand between the feet of those animals, covering themselves with their shields.[34] And since the phalanx of the Moors was of such a sort, the Vandals were at a loss how to handle the situation; for they were neither good with the javelin nor with the bow, nor did they know how to go into battle on foot, but they were all horsemen, and used spears and swords for the most part, so that they were unable to do the enemy any harm at a distance; and their horses, annoyed at the sight of the camels, refused absolutely to be driven against the enemy. And since the Moors, by hurling javelins in great numbers among them from their safe position, kept killing both their horses and men without difficulty, because they were a vast throng, they began to flee, and, when the Moors came out against them, the most of them were destroyed, while some fell into the hands of the enemy; and an exceedingly small number from this army returned home. Such was the fortune which Trasamundus suffered at the hands of the Moors. And he died at a later time, having ruled over the Moors twenty-seven years.


IX


[523 A.D.] And Ilderic, the son of Honoric, the son of Gizeric, next received the kingdom, a ruler who was easily approached by his subjects and altogether gentle, and he shewed himself harsh neither to the Christians nor to anyone else, but in regard to affairs of war he was a weakling and did not wish this thing even to come to his ears. Hoamer, accordingly, his nephew and an able warrior, led the armies against any with whom the Vandals were at war; he it was whom they called the Achilles of the Vandals. During the reign of this Ilderic the Vandals were defeated in Byzacium by the Moors, who were ruled by Antalas, and it so fell out that they became enemies instead of allies and friends to Theoderic and the Goths in Italy. For they put Amalafrida in prison and destroyed all the Goths, charging them with revolutionary designs against the Vandals and Ilderic. However, no revenge came from Theoderic, for he considered himself unable to gather a great fleet and make an expedition into Libya, and Ilderic was a very particular friend and guest-friend of Justinian, who had not yet come to the throne, but was administering the government according to his pleasure; for his uncle Justinus, who was emperor, was very old and not altogether experienced in matters of state. And Ilderic and Justinian made large presents of money to each other.

Now there was a certain man in the family of Gizeric, Gelimer, the son of Geilaris, the son of Genzon, the son of Gizeric, who was of such age as to be second only to Ilderic, and for this reason he was expected to come into the kingdom very soon. This man was thought to be the best warrior of his time, but for the rest he was a cunning fellow and base at heart and well versed in undertaking revolutionary enterprises and in laying hold upon the money of others. Now this Gelimer, when he saw the power coming to him, was not able to live in his accustomed way, but assumed to himself the tasks of a king and usurped the rule, though it was not yet due him; and since Ilderic in a spirit of friendliness gave in to him, he was no longer able to restrain his thoughts, but allying with himself all the noblest of the Vandals, he persuaded them to wrest the kingdom from Ilderic, as being an unwarlike king who had been defeated by the Moors, and as betraying the power of the Vandals into the hand of the Emperor Justinus, in order that the kingdom might not come to him, because he was of the other branch of the family; for he asserted slanderously that this was the meaning of Ilderic's embassy to Byzantium, and that he was giving over the empire of the Vandals to Justinus. And they, being persuaded, carried out this plan. [530 A.D.] Thus Gelimer seized the supreme power, and imprisoned Ilderic, after he had ruled over the Vandals seven years, and also Hoamer and his brother Euagees.

[527 A.D.] But when Justinian heard these things, having already received the imperial power, he sent envoys to Gelimer in Libya with the following letter: "You are not acting in a holy manner nor worthily of the will of Gizeric, keeping in prison an old man and a kinsman and the king of the Vandals (if the counsels of Gizeric are to be of effect), and robbing him of his office by violence, though it would be possible for you to receive it after a short time in a lawful manner. Do you therefore do no further wrong and do not exchange the name of king for the title of tyrant, which comes but a short time earlier. But as for this man, whose death may be expected at any moment, allow him to bear in appearance the form of royal power, while you do all the things which it is proper that a king should do; and wait until you can receive from time and the law of Gizeric, and from them alone, the name which belongs to the position. For if you do this, the attitude of the Almighty will be favourable and at the same time our relations with you will be friendly." Such was his message. But Gelimer sent the envoys away with nothing accomplished, and he blinded Hoamer and also kept Ilderic and Euagees in closer confinement, charging them with planning flight to Byzantium. And when this too was heard by the Emperor Justinian, he sent envoys a second time and wrote as follows: "We, indeed, supposed that you would never go contrary to our advice when we wrote you the former letter. But since it pleases you to have secured possession of the royal power in the manner in which you have taken and now hold it, get from it whatever Heaven grants. But do you send to us Ilderic, and Hoamer whom you have blinded, and his brother, to receive what comfort they can who have been robbed of a kingdom or of sight; for we shall not let the matter rest if you do not do this. And I speak thus because we are led by the hope which I had based on our friendship. And the treaty with Gizeric will not stand as an obstacle for us. For it is not to make war upon him who has succeeded to the kingdom of Gizeric that we come, but to avenge Gizeric with all our power."

When Gelimer had read this, he replied as follows: "King Gelimer to the Emperor Justinian. Neither have I taken the office by violence nor has anything unholy been done by me to my kinsmen. For

Ilderic, while planning a revolution against the house of Gizeric, was dethroned by the nation of the Vandals; and I was called to the kingdom by my years, which gave me the preference, according to the law at least. Now it is well for one to administer the kingly office which belongs to him and not to make the concerns of others his own. Hence for you also, who have a kingdom, meddling in other's affairs is not just; and if you break the treaty and come against us, we shall oppose you with all our power, calling to witness the oaths which were sworn by Zeno, from whom you have received the kingdom which you hold." The Emperor Justinian, upon receiving this letter, having been angry with Gelimer even before then, was still more eager to punish him. And it seemed to him best to put an end to the Persian war as soon as possible and then to make an expedition to Libya; and since he was quick at forming a plan and prompt in carrying out his decisions, Belisarius, the General of the East, was summoned and came to him immediately, no announcement having been made to him nor to anyone else that he was about to lead an army against Libya, but it was given out that he had been removed from the office which he held. And straightway the treaty with Persia was made, as has been told in the preceding narrative.[35]


X


And when the Emperor Justinian considered that the situation was as favourable as possible, both as to domestic affairs and as to his relations with Persia, he took under consideration the situation in Libya. But when he disclosed to the magistrates that he was gathering an army against the Vandals and Gelimer, the most of them began immediately to show hostility to the plan, and they lamented it as a misfortune, recalling the expedition of the Emperor Leon and the disaster of Basiliscus, and reciting how many soldiers had perished and how much money the state had lost. But the men who were the most sorrowful of all, and who, by reason of their anxiety, felt the keenest regret, were the pretorian prefect, whom the Romans call "praetor," and the administrator of the treasury, and all to whom had been assigned the collection of either public or imperial[36] taxes, for they reasoned that while it would be necessary for them to produce countless sums for the needs of the war, they would be granted neither pardon in case of failure nor extension of time in which to raise these sums. And every one of the generals, supposing that he himself would command the army, was in terror and dread at the greatness of the danger, if it should be necessary for him, if he were preserved from the perils of the sea, to encamp in the enemy's land, and, using his ships as a base, to engage in a struggle against a kingdom both large and formidable. The soldiers, also, having recently returned from a long, hard war, and having not yet tasted to the full the blessings of home, were in despair, both because they were being led into sea-fighting, a thing which they had not learned even from tradition before then, and because they were sent from the eastern frontier to the West, in order to risk their lives against Vandals and Moors. But all the rest, as usually happens in a great throng, wished to be spectators of new adventures while others faced the dangers.

But as for saying anything to the emperor to prevent the expedition, no one dared to do this except John the Cappadocian, the pretorian prefect, a man of the greatest daring and the cleverest of all men of his time. For this John, while all the others were bewailing in silence the fortune which was upon them, came before the emperor and spoke as follows: "O Emperor, the good faith which thou dost shew in dealing with thy subjects enables us to speak frankly regarding anything which will be of advantage to thy government, even though what is said and done may not be agreeable to thee. For thus does thy wisdom temper thy authority with justice, in that thou dost not consider that man only as loyal to thy cause who serves thee under any and all conditions, nor art thou angry with the man who speaks against thee, but by weighing all things by pure reason alone, thou hast often shewn that it involves us in no danger to oppose thy purposes. Led by these considerations, O Emperor, I have come to offer this advice, knowing that, though I shall give perhaps offence at the moment, if it so chance, yet in the future the loyalty which I bear you will be made clear, and that for this I shall be able to shew thee as a witness. For if, through not hearkening to my words, thou shalt carry out the war against the Vandals, it will come about, if the struggle is prolonged for thee, that my advice will win renown. For if thou hast confidence that thou wilt conquer the enemy, it is not at all unreasonable that thou shouldst sacrifice the lives of men and expend a vast amount of treasure, and undergo the difficulties of the struggle; for victory, coming at the end, covers up all the calamities of war. But if in reality these things lie on the knees of God, and if it behoves us, taking example from what has happened in the past, to fear the outcome of war, on what grounds is it not better to love a state of quiet rather than the dangers of mortal strife? Thou art purposing to make an expedition against Carthage, to which, if one goes by land, the journey is one of a hundred and forty days, and if one goes by water, he is forced to cross the whole open sea and go to its very end. So that he who brings thee news of what will happen in the camp must needs reach thee a year after the event. And one might add that if thou art victorious over thy enemy, thou couldst not take possession of Libya while Sicily and Italy lie in the hands of others; and at the same time, if any reverse befall thee, O Emperor, the treaty having already been broken by thee, thou wilt bring the danger upon our own land. In fact, putting all in a word, it will not be possible for thee to reap the fruits of victory, and at the same time any reversal of fortune will bring harm to what is well established. It is before an enterprise that wise planning is useful. For when men have failed, repentance is of no avail, but before disaster comes there is no danger in altering plans. Therefore it will be of advantage above all else to make fitting use of the decisive moment."

Thus spoke John; and the Emperor Justinian, hearkening to his words, checked his eager desire for the war. But one of the priests whom they call bishops, who had come from the East, said that he wished to have a word with the emperor. And when he met Justinian, he said that God had visited him in a dream, and bidden him go to the emperor and rebuke him, because, after undertaking the task of protecting the Christians in Libya from tyrants, he had for no good reason become afraid. "And yet," He had said, "I will Myself join with him in waging war and make him lord of Libya." When the emperor heard this, he was no longer able to restrain his purpose, and he began to collect the army and the ships, and to make ready supplies of weapons and of food, and he announced to Belisarius that he should be in readiness, because he was very soon to act as general in Libya. Meanwhile Pudentius, one of the natives of Tripolis in Libya, caused this district to revolt from the Vandals, and sending to the emperor he begged that he should despatch an army to him; for, he said, he would with no trouble win the land for the emperor. And Justinian sent him Tattimuth and an army of no very great size. This force Pudentius joined with his own troops and, the Vandals being absent, he gained possession of the land and made it subject to the emperor. And Gelimer, though wishing to inflict punishment upon Pudentius, found the following obstacle in his way.

There was a certain Godas among the slaves of Gelimer, a Goth by birth, a passionate and energetic fellow possessed of great bodily strength, but appearing to be well-disposed to the cause of his master. To this Godas Gelimer entrusted the island of Sardinia, in order both to guard the island and to pay over the annual tribute. But he neither could digest the prosperity brought by fortune nor had he the spirit to endure it, and so he undertook to establish a tyranny, and he refused to continue the payment of the tribute, and actually detached the island from the Vandals and held it himself. And when he perceived that the Emperor Justinian was eager to make war against Libya and Gelimer, he wrote to him as follows:

"It was neither because I yielded to folly nor because I had suffered anything unpleasant at my master's hands that I turned my thoughts towards rebellion, but seeing the extreme cruelty of the man both toward his kinsmen and toward his subjects, I could not, willingly at least, be reputed to have a share in his inhumanity. For it is better to serve a just king than a tyrant whose commands are unlawful. But do thou join with me to assist in this my effort and send soldiers so that I may be able to ward off my assailants."

And the emperor, on receiving this letter, was pleased, and he sent Eulogius as envoy and wrote a letter praising Godas for his wisdom and his zeal for justice, and he promised an alliance and soldiers and a general, who would be able to guard the island with him and to assist him in every other way, so that no trouble should come to him from the Vandals. But Eulogius, upon coming to Sardinia, found that Godas was assuming the name and wearing the dress of a king and that he had attached a body-guard to his person. And when Godas read the emperor's letter, he said that it was his wish to have soldiers, indeed, come to fight along with him, but as for a commander, he had absolutely no desire for one. And having written to the emperor in this sense, he dismissed Eulogius.

XI

The emperor, meanwhile, not having yet ascertained these things, was preparing four hundred soldiers with Cyril as commander, who were to assist Godas in guarding the island. And with them he also had in readiness the expedition against Carthage, ten thousand foot-soldiers, and five thousand horsemen, gathered from the regular troops and from the "foederati." Now at an earlier time only barbarians were enlisted among the foederati, those, namely, who had come into the Roman political system, not in the condition of slaves, since they had not been conquered by the Romans, but on the basis of complete equality.[37] For the Romans call treaties with their enemies "foedera." But at the present time there is nothing to prevent anyone from assuming this name, since time will by no means consent to keep names attached to the things to which they were formerly applied, but conditions are ever changing about according to the desire of men who control them, and men pay little heed to the meaning which they originally attached to a name. And the commanders of the foederati were Dorotheus, the general of the troops in Armenia, and Solomon, who was acting as manager for the general Belisarius; (such a person the Romans call "domesticus." Now this Solomon was a eunuch, but it was not by the devising of man that he had suffered mutilation, but some accident which befell him while in swaddling clothes had imposed this lot upon him); and there were also Cyprian, Valerian, Martinus, Althias, John, Marcellus, and the Cyril whom I have mentioned above; and the commanders of the regular cavalry were Rufinus and Aïgan, who were of the house of Belisarius, and Barbatus and Pappus, while the regular infantry was commanded by Theodorus, who was surnamed Cteanus, and Terentius, Zaïdus, Marcian, and Sarapis. And a certain John, a native of Epidamnus, which is now called Dyrrachium, held supreme command over all the leaders of infantry. Among all these commanders Solomon was from a place in the East, at the very extremity of the Roman domain, where the city called Daras now stands, and Aïgan was by birth of the Massagetae whom they now call Huns; and the rest were almost all inhabitants of the land of Thrace. And there followed with them also four hundred Eruli, whom Pharas led, and about six hundred barbarian allies from the nation of the Massagetae, all mounted bowmen; these were led by Sinnion and Balas, men endowed with bravery and endurance in the highest degree. And for the whole force five hundred ships were required, no one of which was able to carry more than fifty thousand medimni,[38] nor any one less than three thousand. And in all the vessels together there were thirty thousand sailors, Egyptians and Ionians for the most part, and Cilicians, and one commander was appointed over all the ships, Calonymus of Alexandria. And they had also ships of war prepared as for sea-fighting, to the number of ninety-two, and they were single-banked ships covered by decks, in order that the men rowing them might if possible not be exposed to the bolts of the enemy. Such boats are called "dromones"[39] by those of the present time; for they are able to attain a great speed. In these sailed two thousand men of Byzantium, who were all rowers as well as fighting men; for there was not a single superfluous man among them. And Archelaus was also sent, a man of patrician standing who had already been pretorian prefect both in Byzantium and in Illyricum, but he then held the position of prefect of the army; for thus the officer charged with the maintenance of the army is designated. But as general with supreme authority over all the emperor sent Belisarius, who was in command of the troops of the East for the second time. And he was followed by many spearmen and many guards as well, men who were capable warriors and thoroughly experienced in the dangers of fighting. And the emperor gave him written instructions, bidding him do everything as seemed best to him, and stating that his acts would be final, as if the emperor himself had done them. The writing, in fact, gave him the power of a king. Now Belisarius was a native of Germania, which lies between Thrace and Illyricum. These things, then, took place in this way.

Gelimer, however, being deprived of Tripolis by Pudentius and of Sardinia by Godas, scarcely hoped to regain Tripolis, since it was situated at a great distance and the rebels were already being assisted by the Romans, against whom just at that moment it seemed to him best not to take the field; but he was eager to get to the island before any army sent by the emperor to fight for his enemies should arrive there. He accordingly selected five thousand of the Vandals and one hundred and twenty ships of the fastest kind, and appointing as general his brother Tzazon, he sent them off. And so they were sailing with great enthusiasm and eagerness against Godas and Sardinia. In the meantime the Emperor Justinian was sending off Valerian and Martinus in advance of the others in order to await the rest of the army in the Peloponnesus. And when these two had embarked upon their ships, it came to the emperor's mind that there was something which he wished to enjoin upon them, a thing which he had wished to say previously, but he had been so busied with the other matters of which he had to speak that his mind had been occupied with them and this subject had been driven out. He summoned them, accordingly, intending to say what he wished, but upon considering the matter, he saw that it would not be propitious for them to interrupt their journey. He therefore sent men to forbid them either to return to him or to disembark from their ships. And these men, upon coming near the ships, commanded them with much shouting and loud cries by no means to turn back, and it seemed to those present that the thing which had happened was no good omen and that never would one of the men in those ships return from Libya to Byzantium. For besides the omen they suspected that a curse also had come to the men from the emperor, not at all by his own will, so that they would not return. Now if anyone should so interpret the incident with regard to these two commanders, Valerian and Martinus, he will find the original opinion untrue. But there was a certain man among the body-guards of Martinus, Stotzas by name, who was destined to be an enemy of the emperor, to make an attempt to set up a tyranny, and by no means to return to Byzantium, and one might suppose that curse to have been turned upon him by Heaven. But whether this matter stands thus or otherwise, I leave to each one to reason out as he wishes. But I shall proceed to tell how the general Belisarius and the army departed.

XII

[533 A.D.] In the seventh year of Justinian's reign, at about the spring equinox, the emperor commanded the general's ship to anchor off the point which is before the royal palace. Thither came also Epiphanius, the chief priest of the city, and after uttering an appropriate prayer, he put on the ships one of the soldiers who had lately been baptized and had taken the Christian name. And after this the general Belisarius and Antonina, his wife, set sail. And there was with them also Procopius, who wrote this history; now previously he had been exceedingly terrified at the danger, but later he had seen a vision in his sleep which caused him to take courage and made him eager to go on the expedition. For it seemed in the dream that he was in the house of Belisarius, and one of the servants entering announced that some men had come bearing gifts; and Belisarius bade him investigate what sort of gifts they were, and he went out into the court and saw men who carried on their shoulders earth with the flowers and all. And he bade him bring these men into the house and deposit the earth they were carrying in the portico; and Belisarius together with his guardsmen came there, and he himself reclined on that earth and ate of the flowers, and urged the others to do likewise; and as they reclined and ate, as if upon a couch, the food seemed to them exceedingly sweet. Such, then, was the vision of the dream.

And the whole fleet followed the general's ship, and they put in at Perinthus, which is now called Heracleia,[40] where five days' time was spent by the army, since at that place the general received as a present from the emperor an exceedingly great number of horses from the royal pastures, which are kept for him in the territory of Thrace. And setting sail from there, they anchored off Abydus, and it came about as they were delaying there four days on account of the lack of wind that the following event took place. Two Massagetae killed one of their comrades who was ridiculing them, in the midst of their intemperate drinking; for they were intoxicated. For of all men the Massagetae are the most intemperate drinkers. Belisarius, accordingly, straightway impaled these two men on the hill which is near Abydus. And since all, and especially the relatives of these two men, were angry and declared that it was not in order to be punished nor to be subject to the laws of the Romans that they had entered into an alliance (for their own laws did not make the punishment for murder such as this, they said); and since they were joined in voicing the accusation against the general even by Roman soldiers, who were anxious that there should be no punishment for their offences, Belisarius called together both the Massagetae and the rest of the army and spoke as follows: "If my words were addressed to men now for the first time entering into war, it would require a long time for me to convince you by speech how great a help justice is for gaining the victory. For those who do not understand the fortunes of such struggles think that the outcome of war lies in strength of arm alone. But you, who have often conquered an enemy not inferior to you in strength of body and well endowed with valour, you who have often tried your strength against your opponents, you, I think, are not ignorant that, while it is men who always do the fighting in either army, it is God who judges the contest as seems best to Him and bestows the victory in battle. Now since this is so, it is fitting to consider good bodily condition and practice in arms and all the other provision for war of less account than justice and those things which pertain to God. For that which may possibly be of greatest advantage to men in need would naturally be honoured by them above all other things. Now the first proof of justice would be the punishment of those who have committed unjust murder. For if it is incumbent upon us to sit in judgment upon the actions which from time to time are committed by men toward their neighbours, and to adjudge and to name the just and the unjust action, we should find that nothing is more precious to a man than his life. And if any barbarian who has slain his kinsman expects to find indulgence in his trial on the ground that he was drunk, in all fairness he makes the charge so much the worse by reason of the very circumstance by which, as he alleges, his guilt is removed. For it is not right for a man under any circumstances, and especially when serving in an army, to be so drunk as readily to kill his dearest friends; nay, the drunkenness itself, even if the murder is not added at all, is worthy of punishment; and when a kinsman is wronged, the crime would clearly be of greater moment as regards punishment than when committed against those who are not kinsmen, at least in the eyes of men of sense. Now the example is before you and you may see what sort of an outcome such actions have. But as for you, it is your duty to avoid laying violent hands upon anyone without provocation, or carrying off the possessions of others; for I shall not overlook it, be assured, and I shall not consider anyone of you a fellow-soldier of mine, no matter how terrible he is reputed to be to the foe, who is not able to use clean hands against the enemy. For bravery cannot be victorious unless it be arrayed along with justice." So spoke Belisarius. And the whole army, hearing what was said and looking up at the two men impaled, felt an overwhelming fear come over them and took thought to conduct their lives with moderation, for they saw that they would not be free from great danger if they should be caught doing anything unlawful.

XIII

After this Belisarius bethought him how his whole fleet should always keep together as it sailed and should anchor in the same place. For he knew that in a large fleet, and especially if rough winds should assail them, it was inevitable that many of the ships should be left behind and scattered on the open sea, and that their pilots should not know which of the ships that put to sea ahead of them it was better to follow. So after considering the matter, he did as follows. The sails of the three ships in which he and his following were carried he painted red from the upper corner for about one third of their length, and he erected upright poles on the prow of each, and hung lights from them, so that both by day and by night the general's ships might be distinguishable; then he commanded all the pilots to follow these ships. Thus with the three ships leading the whole fleet not a single ship was left behind. And whenever they were about to put out from a harbour, the trumpets announced this to them.

And upon setting out from Abydus they met with strong winds which carried them to Sigeum. And again in calm weather they proceeded more leisurely to Malea, where the calm proved of the greatest advantage to them. For since they had a great fleet and exceedingly large ships, as night came on everything was thrown into confusion by reason of their being crowded into small space, and they were brought into extreme peril. At that time both the pilots and the rest of the sailors shewed themselves skilful and efficient, for while shouting at the top of their voices and making a great noise they kept pushing the ships apart with their poles, and cleverly kept the distances between their different vessels; but if a wind had arisen, whether a following or a head wind, it seems to me that the sailors would hardly have preserved themselves and their ships. But as it was, they escaped, as I have said, and put in at Taenarum, which is now called Caenopolis.[41] Then, pressing on from there, they touched at Methone, and found Valerian and Martinus with their men, who had reached the same place a short time before. And since there were no winds blowing, Belisarius anchored the ships there, and disembarked the whole army; and after they were on shore he assigned the commanders their positions and drew up the soldiers. And while he was thus engaged and no wind at all arose, it came about that many of the soldiers were destroyed by disease caused in the following manner.

The pretorian prefect, John, was a man of worthless character, and so skilful at devising ways of bringing money into the public treasury to the detriment of men that I, for my part, should never be competent to describe this trait of his. But this has been said in the preceding pages, when I was brought to this point by my narrative.[42] But I shall tell in the present case in what manner he destroyed the soldiers. The bread which soldiers are destined to eat in camp must of necessity be put twice into the oven, and be cooked so carefully as to last for a very long period and not spoil in a short time, and loaves cooked in this way necessarily weigh less; and for this reason, when such bread is distributed, the soldiers generally received as their portion one-fourth more than the usual weight.[43] John, therefore, calculating how he might reduce the amount of firewood used and have less to pay to the bakers in wages, and also how he might not lose in the weight of the bread, brought the still uncooked dough to the public baths of Achilles, in the basement of which the fire is kept burning, and bade his men set it down there. And when it seemed to be cooked in some fashion or other, he threw it into bags, put it on the ships, and sent it off. And when the fleet arrived at Methone, the loaves disintegrated and returned again to flour, not wholesome flour, however, but rotten and becoming mouldy and already giving out a sort of oppressive odour. And the loaves were dispensed by measure[44] to the soldiers by those to whom this office was assigned, and they were already making the distribution of the bread by quarts and bushels. And the soldiers, feeding upon this in the summer time in a place where the climate is very hot, became sick, and not less than five hundred of them died; and the same thing was about to happen to more, but Belisarius prevented it by ordering the bread of the country to be furnished them. And reporting the matter to the emperor, he himself gained in favour, but he did not at that time bring any punishment upon John.

These events, then, took place in the manner described. And setting out from Methone they reached the harbour of Zacynthus, where they took in enough water to last them in crossing the Adriatic Sea, and after making all their other preparations, sailed on. But since the wind they had was very gentle and languid, it was only on the sixteenth day that they came to land at a deserted place in Sicily near which Mount Aetna rises. And while they were being delayed in this passage, as has been said, it so happened that the water of the whole fleet was spoiled, except that which Belisarius himself and his table-companions were drinking. For this alone was preserved by the wife of Belisarius in the following manner. She filled with water jars made of glass and constructed a small room with planks in the hold of the ship where it was impossible for the sun to penetrate, and there she sank the jars in sand, and by this means the water remained unaffected. So much, then, for this.


XIV

And as soon as Belisarius had disembarked upon the island, he began to feel restless, knowing not how to proceed, and his mind was tormented by the thought that he did not know what sort of men the Vandals were against whom he was going, and how strong they were in war, or in what manner the Romans would have to wage the war, or what place would be their base of operations. But most of all he was disturbed by the soldiers, who were in mortal dread of sea-fighting and had no shame in saying beforehand that, if they should be disembarked on the land, they would try to show themselves brave men in the battle, but if hostile ships assailed them, they would turn to flight; for, they said, they were not able to contend against two enemies at once, both men and water. Being at a loss, therefore, because of all these things, he sent Procopius, his adviser, to Syracuse, to find out whether the enemy had any ships in ambush keeping watch over the passage across the sea, either on the island or on the continent, and where it would be best for them to anchor in Libya, and from what point as base it would be advantageous for them to start in carrying on the war against the Vandals. And he bade him, when he should have accomplished his commands, return and meet him at the place called Caucana,[45] about two hundred stades distant from Syracuse, where both he and the whole fleet were to anchor. But he let it be understood that he was sending him to buy provisions, since the Goths were willing to give them a market, this having been decided upon by the Emperor Justinian and Amalasountha, the mother of Antalaric,[46] who was at that time a boy being reared under the care of his mother, Amalasountha, and held sway over both the Goths and the Italians. For when Theoderic had died and the kingdom came to his nephew, Antalaric, who had already before this lost his father, Amalasountha was fearful both for her child and for the kingdom and cultivated the friendship of Justinian very carefully, and she gave heed to his commands in all matters and at that time promised to provide a market for his army and did so.

Now when Procopius reached Syracuse, he unexpectedly met a man who had been a fellow-citizen and friend of his from childhood, who had been living in Syracuse for a long time engaged in the shipping business, and he learned from him what he wanted; for this man showed him a domestic who had three days before that very day come from Carthage, and he said that they need not suspect that there would be any ambush set for the fleet by the Vandals. For from no one in the world had they learned that an army was coming against them at that time, but all the active men among the Vandals had actually a little before gone on an expedition against Godas. And for this reason Gelimer, with no thought of an enemy in his mind and regardless of Carthage and all the other places on the sea, was staying in Hermione, which is in Byzacium, four days' journey distant from the coast; so that it was possible for them to sail without fearing any difficulty and to anchor wherever the wind should call them. When Procopius heard this, he took the hand of the domestic and walked to the harbour of Arethousa where his boat lay at anchor, making many enquiries of the man and searching out every detail. And going on board the ship with him, he gave orders to raise the sails and to make all speed for Caucana. And since the master of the domestic stood on the shore wondering that he did not give him back the man, Procopius shouted out, when the ship was already under way, begging him not to be angry with him; for it was necessary that the domestic should meet the general, and, after leading the army to Libya, would return after no long time to Syracuse with much money in his pocket.

But upon coming to Caucana they found all in deep grief. For Dorotheus, the general of the troops of Armenia, had died there, leaving to the whole army a great sense of loss. But Belisarius, when the domestic had come before him and related his whole story, became exceedingly glad, and after bestowing many praises upon Procopius, he issued orders to give the signal for departure with the trumpets. And setting sail quickly they touched at the islands of Gaulus and Melita,[47] which mark the boundary between the Adriatic and Tuscan Seas. There a strong east wind arose for them, and on the following day it carried the ships to the point of Libya, at the place which the Romans call in their own tongue "Shoal's Head." For its name is "Caputvada," and it is five days' journey from Carthage for an unencumbered traveller.


XV

And when they came near the shore, the general bade them furl the sails, throw out anchors from the ships, and make a halt; and calling together all the commanders to his own ship, he opened a discussion with regard to the disembarkation. Thereupon many speeches were made inclining to either side, and Archelaus came forward and spoke as follows:

"I admire, indeed, the virtue of our general, who, while surpassing all by far in judgment and possessing the greatest wealth of experience, and at the same time holding the power alone, has proposed an open discussion and bids each one of us speak, so that we shall be able to choose whichever course seems best, though it is possible for him to decide alone on what is needful and at his leisure to put it into execution as he wishes. But as for you, my fellow officers, I do not know how I am to say it easily, one might wonder that each one did not hasten to be the first to oppose the disembarkation. And yet I understand that the making of suggestions to those who are entering upon a perilous course brings no personal advantage to him who offers the advice, but as a general thing results in bringing blame upon him. For when things go well for men, they attribute their success to their own judgment or to fortune, but when they fail, they blame only the one who has advised them. Nevertheless I shall speak out. For it is not right for those who deliberate about safety to shrink from blame. You are purposing to disembark on the enemy's land, fellow-officers; but in what harbour are you planning to place the ships in safety? Or in what city's wall will you find security for yourselves? Have you not then heard that this promontory, I mean from Carthage to Iouce, extends, they say, for a journey of nine days, altogether without harbours and lying open to the wind from whatever quarter it may blow? And not a single walled town is left in all Libya except Carthage, thanks to the decision of Gizeric.[48] And one might add that in this place, they say, water is entirely lacking. Come now, if you wish, let us suppose that some adversity befall us, and with this in view make the decision. For that those who enter into contests of arms should expect no difficulty is not in keeping with human experience nor with the nature of things. If, then, after we have disembarked upon the mainland, a storm should fall upon us, will it not be necessary that one of two things befall the ships, either that they flee away as far as possible, or perish upon this promontory? Secondly, what means will there be of supplying us with necessities? Let no one look to me as the officer charged with the maintenance of the army. For every official, when deprived of the means of administering his office, is of necessity reduced to the name and character of a private person. And where shall we deposit our superfluous arms or any other part of our necessaries when we are compelled to receive the attack of the barbarians? Nay, as for this, it is not well even to say how it will turn out. But I think that we ought to make straight for Carthage. For they say that there is a harbour called Stagnum not more than forty stades distant from that city, which is entirely unguarded and large enough for the whole fleet. And if we make this the base of our operations, we shall carry on the war without difficulty. And I, for my part, think it likely that we shall win Carthage by a sudden attack, especially since the enemy are far away from it, and that after we have won it we shall have no further trouble. For it is a way with all men's undertakings that when the chief point has been captured, they collapse after no long time. It behoves us, therefore, to bear in mind all these things and to choose the best course." So spoke Archelaus.

And Belisarius spoke as follows: "Let no one of you, fellow-officers, think that my words are those of censure, nor that they are spoken in the last place to the end that it may become necessary for all to follow them, of whatever sort they may be. For I have heard what seems best to each one of you, and it is becoming that I too should lay before you what I think, and then with you should choose the better course. But it is right to remind you of this fact, that the soldiers said openly a little earlier that they feared the dangers by sea and would turn to flight if a hostile ship should attack them, and we prayed God to shew us the land of Libya and allow us a peaceful disembarkation upon it. And since this is so, I think it the part of foolish men first to pray to receive from God the more favourable fortune, then when this is given them, to reject it and go in the contrary direction. And if we do sail straight for Carthage and a hostile fleet encounters us, the soldiers will remain without blame, if they flee with all their might, for a delinquency announced beforehand carries with it its own defence, but for us, even if we come through safely, there will be no forgiveness. Now while there are many difficulties if we remain in the ships, it will be sufficient, I think, to mention only one thing, that by which especially they wish to frighten us when they hold over our heads the danger of a storm. For if any storm should fall upon us, one of two things, they say, must necessarily befall the ships, either that they flee far from Libya or be destroyed upon this headland. What then under the present circumstances will be more to our advantage to choose? to have the ships alone destroyed, or to have lost everything, men and all? But apart from this, at the present time we shall fall upon the enemy unprepared, and in all probability shall fare as we desire; for in warfare it is the unexpected which is accustomed to govern the course of events. But a little later, when the enemy have already made their preparation, the struggle we shall have will be one of strength evenly matched. And one might add that it will be necessary perhaps to fight even for the disembarkation, and to seek for that which now we have within our grasp but over which we are deliberating as a thing not necessary. And if at the very time, when we are engaged in conflict, a storm also comes upon us, as often happens on the sea, then while struggling both against the waves and against the Vandals, we shall come to regret our prudence. As for me, then, I say that we must disembark upon the land with all possible speed, landing horses and arms and whatever else we consider necessary for our use, and that we must dig a trench quickly and throw a stockade around us of a kind which can contribute to our safety no less than any walled town one might mention, and with that as our base must carry on the war from there if anyone should attack us. And if we shew ourselves brave men, we shall lack nothing in the way of provisions. For those who hold the mastery over their enemy are lords also of the enemy's possessions; and it is the way of victory, first to invest herself with all the wealth, and then to set it down again on that side to which she inclines. Therefore, for you both the chance of safety and of having an abundance of good things lies in your own hands."

When Belisarius had said this, the whole assembly agreed and adopted his proposal, and separating from one another, they made the disembarkation as quickly as possible, about three months later than their departure from Byzantium. And indicating a certain spot on the shore the general bade both soldiers and sailors dig the trench and place the stockade about it. And they did as directed. And since a great throng was working and fear was stimulating their enthusiasm and the general was urging them on, not only was the trench dug on the same day, but the stockade was also completed and the pointed stakes were fixed in place all around. Then, indeed, while they were digging the trench, something happened which was altogether amazing. A great abundance of water sprang forth from the earth, a thing which had not happened before in Byzacium, and besides this the place where they were was altogether waterless. Now this water sufficed for all uses of both men and animals. And in congratulating the general, Procopius said that he rejoiced at the abundance of water, not so much because of its usefulness, as because it seemed to him a symbol of an easy victory, and that Heaven was foretelling a victory to them. This, at any rate, actually came to pass. So for that night all the soldiers bivouacked in the camp, setting guards and doing everything else as was customary, except, indeed, that Belisarius commanded five bowmen to remain in each ship for the purpose of a guard, and that the ships-of-war should anchor in a circle about them, taking care that no one should come against them to do them harm.

XVI

But on the following day, when some of the soldiers went out into the fields and laid hands on the fruit, the general inflicted corporal punishment of no casual sort upon them, and he called all the army together and spoke as follows: "This using of violence and the eating of that which belongs to others seems at other times a wicked thing only on this account, that injustice is in the deed itself, as the saying is; but in the present instance so great an element of detriment is added to the wrongdoing that, if it is not too harsh to say so, we must consider the question of justice of less account and calculate the magnitude of the danger that may arise from your act. For I have disembarked you upon this land basing my confidence on this alone, that the Libyans, being Romans from of old, are unfaithful and hostile to the Vandals, and for this reason I thought that no necessaries would fail us and, besides, that the enemy would not do us any injury by a sudden attack. But now this your lack of self-control has changed it all and made the opposite true. For you have doubtless reconciled the Libyans to the Vandals, bringing their hostility round upon your own selves. For by nature those who are wronged feel enmity toward those who have done them violence, and it has come round to this that you have exchanged your own safety and a bountiful supply of good things for some few pieces of silver, when it was possible for you, by purchasing provisions from willing owners, not to appear unjust and at the same time to enjoy their friendship to the utmost. Now, therefore, the war will be between you and both Vandals and Libyans, and I, at least, say further that it will be against God himself, whose aid no one who does wrong can invoke. But do you cease trespassing wantonly upon the possessions of others, and reject a gain which is full of dangers. For this is that time in which above all others moderation is able to save, but lawlessness leads to death. For if you give heed to these things, you will find God propitious, the Libyan people well-disposed, and the race of the Vandals open to your attack."

With these words Belisarius dismissed the assembly. And at that time he heard that the city of Syllectus was distant one day's journey from the camp, lying close to the sea on the road leading to Carthage, and that the wall of this city had been torn down for a long time, but the inhabitants of the place had made a barrier on all sides by means of the walls of their houses, on account of the attacks of the Moors, and guarded a kind of fortified enclosure; he, accordingly, sent one of his spearmen, Boriades, together with some of the guards, commanding them to make an attempt oh the city, and, if they captured it, to do no harm in it, but to promise a thousand good things and to say that they had come for the sake of the people's freedom, that so the army might be able to enter into it. And they came near the city about dusk and passed the night hidden in a ravine. But at early dawn, meeting country folk going into the city with waggons, they entered quietly with them and with no trouble took possession of the city. And when day came, no one having begun any disturbance, they called together the priest and all the other notables and announced the commands of the general, and receiving the keys of the entrances from willing hands, they sent them to the general.

On the same day the overseer of the public post deserted, handing over all the government horses. And they captured also one of those who are occasionally sent to bear the royal responses, whom they call "veredarii"[49]; and the general did him no harm but presented him with much gold and, receiving pledges from him, put into his hand the letter which the Emperor Justinian had written to the Vandals, that he might give it to the magistrates of the Vandals. And the writing was as follows: "Neither have we decided to make war upon the Vandals, nor are we breaking the treaty of Gizeric, but we are attempting to dethrone your tyrant, who, making light of the testament of Gizeric, has imprisoned your king and is keeping him in custody, and those of his relatives whom he hated exceedingly he put to death at the first, and the rest, after robbing them of their sight, he keeps under guard, not allowing them to terminate their misfortunes by death. Do you, therefore, join forces with us and help us in freeing yourselves from so wicked a tyranny, in order that you may be able to enjoy both peace and freedom. For we give you pledges in the name of God that these things will come to you by our hand." Such was the message of the emperor's letter. But the man who received this from Belisarius did not dare to publish it openly, and though he shewed it secretly to his friends, he accomplished nothing whatever of consequence.

XVII

And Belisarius, having arrayed his army as for battle in the following manner, began the march to Carthage. He chose out three hundred of his guards, men who were able warriors, and handed them over to John, who was in charge of the expenditures of the general's household; such a person the Romans call "optio."[50] And he was an Armenian by birth, a man gifted with discretion and courage in the highest degree. This John, then, he commanded to go ahead of the army, at a distance of not less than twenty stades, and if he should see anything of the enemy, to report it with all speed, so that they might not be compelled to enter into battle unprepared. And the allied Massagetae he commanded to travel constantly on the left of the army, keeping as many stades away or more; and he himself marched in the rear with the best troops. For he suspected that it would not be long before Gelimer, following them from Hermione, would make an attack upon them. And these precautions were sufficient, for on the right side there was no fear, since they were travelling not far from the coast. And he commanded the sailors to follow along with them always and not to separate themselves far from the army, but when the wind was favouring to lower the great sails, and follow with the small sails, which they call "dolones,"[51] and when the wind dropped altogether to keep the ships under way as well as they could by rowing.

And when Belisarius reached Syllectus, the soldiers behaved with moderation, and they neither began any unjust brawls nor did anything out of the way, and he himself, by displaying great gentleness and kindness, won the Libyans to his side so completely that thereafter he made the journey as if in his own land; for neither did the inhabitants of the land withdraw nor did they wish to conceal anything, but they both furnished a market and served the soldiers in whatever else they wished. And accomplishing eighty stades each day, we completed the whole journey to Carthage, passing the night either in a city, should it so happen, or in a camp made as thoroughly secure as the circumstances permitted. Thus we passed through the city of Leptis and Hadrumetum and reached the place called Grasse, three hundred and fifty stades distant from Carthage. In that place was a palace of the ruler of the Vandals and a park the most beautiful of all we know. For it is excellently watered by springs and has a great wealth of woods. And all the trees are full of fruit; so that each one of the soldiers pitched his tent among fruit-trees, and though all of them ate their fill of the fruit, which was then ripe, there was practically no diminution to be seen in the fruit.

But Gelimer, as soon as he heard in Hermione that the enemy were at hand, wrote to his brother Ammatas in Carthage to kill Ilderic and all the others, connected with him either by birth or otherwise, whom he was keeping under guard, and commanded him to make ready the Vandals and all others in the city serviceable for war, in order that, when the enemy got inside the narrow passage at the suburb of the city which they call Decimum,[52] they might come together from both sides and surround them and, catching them as in a net, destroy them. And Ammatas carried this out, and killed Ilderic, who was a relative of his, and Euagees, and all the Libyans who were intimate with them. For Hoamer had already departed from the world.[53] And arming the Vandals, he made them ready, intending to make his attack at the opportune moment. But Gelimer was following behind, without letting it be known to us, except, indeed, that, on that night when we bivouacked in Grasse, scouts coming from both armies met each other, and after an exchange of blows they each retired to their own camp, and in this way it became evident to us that the enemy were not far away. As we proceeded from there it was impossible to discern the ships. For high rocks extending well into the sea cause mariners to make a great circuit, and there is a projecting headland,[54] inside of which lies the town of Hermes. Belisarius therefore commanded Archelaus, the prefect, and Calonymus, the admiral, not to put in at Carthage, but to remain about two hundred stades away until he himself should summon them. And departing from Grasse we came on the fourth day to Decimum, seventy stades distant from Carthage.


XVIII

And on that day Gelimer commanded his nephew Gibamundus with two thousand of the Vandals to go ahead of the rest of the army on the left side, in order that Ammatas coming from Carthage, Gelimer himself from the rear, and Gibamundus from the country to the left, might unite and accomplish the task of encircling the enemy with less difficulty and exertion. But as for me, during this struggle I was moved to wonder at the ways of Heaven and of men, noting how God, who sees from afar what will come to pass, traces out the manner in which it seems best to him that things should come to pass, while men, whether they are deceived or counsel aright, know not that they have failed, should that be the issue, or that they have succeeded, God's purpose being that a path shall be made for Fortune, who presses on inevitably toward that which has been foreordained. For if Belisarius had not thus arranged his forces, commanding the men under John to take the lead, and the Massagetae to march on the left of the army, we should never have been able to escape the Vandals. And even with this planned so by Belisarius, if Ammatas had observed the opportune time, and had not anticipated this by about the fourth part of a day, never would the cause of the Vandals have fallen as it did; but as it was, Ammatas came to Decimum about midday, in advance of the time, while both we and the Vandal army were far away, erring not only in that he did not arrive at the fitting time, but also in leaving at Carthage the host of the Vandals, commanding them to come to Decimum as quickly as possible, while he with a few men and not even the pick of the army came into conflict with John's men. And he killed twelve of the best men who were fighting in the front rank, and he himself fell, having shewn himself a brave man in this engagement. And the rout, after Ammatas fell, became complete, and the Vandals, fleeing at top speed, swept back all those who were coming from Carthage to Decimum. For they were advancing in no order and not drawn up as for battle, but in companies, and small ones at that; for they were coming in bands of twenty or thirty. And seeing the Vandals under Ammatas fleeing, and thinking their pursuers were a great multitude, they turned and joined in the flight. And John and his men, killing all whom they came upon, advanced as far as the gates of Carthage. And there was so great a slaughter of Vandals in the course of the seventy stades that those who beheld it would have supposed that it was the work of an enemy twenty thousand strong.

At the same time Gibamundus and his two thousand came to Pedion Halon, which is forty stades distant from Decimum on the left as one goes to Carthage, and is destitute of human habitation or trees or anything else, since the salt in the water permits nothing except salt to be produced there; in that place they encountered the Huns and were all destroyed. Now there was a certain man among the Massagetae, well gifted with courage and strength of body, the leader of a few men; this man had the privilege handed down from his fathers and ancestors to be the first in all the Hunnic armies to attack the enemy. For it was not lawful for a man of the Massagetae to strike first in battle and capture one of the enemy until, indeed, someone from this house began the struggle with the enemy. So when the two armies had come not far from each other, this man rode out and stopped alone close to the army of the Vandals. And the Vandals, either because they were dumbfounded at the courageous spirit of the man or perhaps because they suspected that the enemy were contriving something against them, decided neither to move nor to shoot at the man. And I think that, since they had never had experience of battle with the Massagetae, but heard that the nation was very warlike, they were for this reason terrified at the danger. And the man, returning to his compatriots, said that God had sent them these strangers as a ready feast. Then at length they made their onset and the Vandals did not withstand them, but breaking their ranks and never thinking of resistance, they were all disgracefully destroyed.

## XIX

But we, having learned nothing at all of what had happened, were going on to Decimum. And Belisarius, seeing a place well adapted for a camp, thirty-five stades distant from Decimum, surrounded it with a stockade which was very well made, and placing all the infantry there and calling together the whole army, he spoke as follows: "Fellow-soldiers, the decisive moment of the struggle is already at hand; for I perceive that the enemy are advancing upon us; and the ships have been taken far away from us by the nature of the place; and it has come round to this that our hope of safety lies in the strength of our hands. For there is not a friendly city, no, nor any other stronghold, in which we may put our trust and have confidence concerning ourselves. But if we should show ourselves brave men, it is probable that we shall still overcome the enemy in the war; but if we should weaken at all, it will remain for us to fall under the hand of the Vandals and to be destroyed disgracefully. And yet there are many advantages on our side to help us on toward victory; for we have with us both justice, with which we have come against our enemy (for we are here in order to recover what is our own), and the hatred of the Vandals toward their own tyrant. For the alliance of God follows naturally those who put justice forward, and a soldier who is ill-disposed toward his ruler knows not how to play the part of a brave man. And apart from this, we have been engaged with Persians and Scythians all the time, but the Vandals, since the time they conquered Libya, have seen not a single enemy except naked Moors. And who does not know that in every work practice leads to skill, while idleness leads to inefficiency? Now the stockade, from which we shall have to carry on the war, has been made by us in the best possible manner. And we are able to deposit here our weapons and everything else which we are not able to carry when we go forth; and when we return here again, no kind of provisions can fail us. And I pray that each one of you, calling to mind his own valour and those whom he has left at home, may so march with contempt against the enemy."

After speaking these words and uttering a prayer after them, Belisarius left his wife and the barricaded camp to the infantry, and himself set forth with all the horsemen. For it did not seem to him advantageous for the present to risk an engagement with the whole army, but it seemed wise to skirmish first with the horsemen and make trial of the enemy's strength, and finally to fight a decisive battle with the whole army. Sending forward, therefore, the commanders of the foederati,[55] he himself followed with the rest of the force and his own spearmen and guards. And when the foederati and their leaders reached Decimum, they saw the corpses of the fallen, twelve comrades from the forces of John and near them Ammatas and some of the Vandals. And hearing from the inhabitants of the place the whole story of the fight, they were vexed, being at a loss as to where they ought to go. But while they were still at a loss and from the hills were looking around over the whole country thereabouts, a dust appeared from the south and a little later a very large force of Vandal horsemen. And they sent to Belisarius urging him to come as quickly as possible, since the enemy were bearing down upon them. And the opinions of the commanders were divided. For some thought that they ought to close with their assailants, but the others said that their force was not sufficient for this. And while they were debating thus among themselves, the barbarians drew near under the leadership of Gelimer, who was following a road between the one which Belisarius was travelling and the one by which the Massagetae who had encountered Gibamundus had come. But since the land was hilly on both sides, it did not allow him to see either the disaster of Gibamundus or Belisarius' stockade, nor even the road along which Belisarius' men were advancing. But when they came near each other, a contest arose between the two armies as to which should capture the highest of all the hills there. For it seemed a suitable one to encamp upon, and both sides preferred to engage with the enemy from there. And the Vandals, coming first, took possession of the hill by crowding off their assailants and routed the enemy, having already become an object of terror to them. And the Romans in flight came to a place seven stades distant from Decimum, where, as it happened, Uliaris, the personal guard of Belisarius, was, with eight hundred guardsmen. And all supposed that Uliaris would receive them and hold his position, and together with them would go against the Vandals; but when they came together, these troops all unexpectedly fled at top speed and went on the run to Belisarius.

From then on I am unable to say what happened to Gelimer that, having the victory in his hands, he willingly gave it up to the enemy, unless one ought to refer foolish actions also to God, who, whenever He purposes that some adversity shall befall a man, touches first his reason and does not permit that which will be to his advantage to come to his consideration. For if, on the one hand, he had made the pursuit immediately, I do not think that even Belisarius would have withstood him, but our cause would have been utterly and completely lost, so numerous appeared the force of the Vandals and so great the fear they inspired in the Romans; or if, on the other hand, he had even ridden straight for Carthage, he would easily have killed all John's men, who, heedless of everything else, were wandering about the plain one by one or by twos and stripping the dead. And he would have preserved the city with its treasures, and captured our ships, which had come rather near, and he would have withdrawn from us all hope both of sailing away and of victory. But in fact he did neither of these things. Instead he descended from the hill at a walk, and when he reached the level ground and saw the corpse of his brother, he turned to lamentations, and, in caring for his burial, he blunted the edge of his opportunity, an opportunity which he was not able to grasp again. Meantime Belisarius, meeting the fugitives, bade them stop, and arrayed them all in order and rebuked them at length; then, after hearing of the death of Ammatas and the pursuit of John, and learning what he wished concerning the place and the enemy, he proceeded at full speed against Gelimer and the Vandals. But the barbarians, having already fallen into disorder and being now unprepared, did not withstand the onset of the Romans, but fled with all their might, losing many there, and the battle ended at night. Now the Vandals were in flight, not to Carthage nor to Byzacium, whence they had come, but to the plain of Boulla and the road leading into Numidia. So the men with John and the Massagetae returned to us about dusk, and after learning all that had happened and reporting what they had done, they passed the night with us in Decimum.

XX

But on the following day the infantry with the wife of Belisarius came up and we all proceeded together on the road toward Carthage, which we reached in the late evening; and we passed the night in the open, although no one hindered us from marching into the city at once. For the Carthaginians opened the gates and burned lights everywhere and the city was brilliant with the illumination that whole night, and those of the Vandals who had been left behind were sitting as suppliants in the sanctuaries. But Belisarius prevented the entrance in order to guard against any ambuscade being set for his men by the enemy, and also to prevent the soldiers from having freedom to turn to plundering, as they might under the concealment of night. On that day, since an east wind arose for them, the ships reached the headland, and the Carthaginians, for they already sighted them, removed the iron chains of the harbour which they call Mandracium, and made it possible for the fleet to enter. Now there is in the king's palace a room filled with darkness, which the Carthaginians call Ancon, where all were cast with whom the tyrant was angry. In that place, as it happened, many of the eastern merchants had been confined up to that time. For Gelimer was angry with these men, charging them with having urged the emperor on to the war, and they were about to be destroyed, all of them, this having been decided upon by Gelimer on that day on which Ammatas was killed in Decimum; to such an extremity of danger did they come. The guard of this prison, upon hearing what had taken place in Decimum and seeing the fleet inside the point, entered the room and enquired of the men, who had not yet learned the good news, but were sitting in the darkness and expecting death, what among their possessions they would be willing to give up and be saved. And when they said they desired to give everything he might wish, he demanded nothing of all their treasures, but required them all to swear that, if they escaped, they would assist him also with all their power when he came into danger. And they did this. Then he told them them the whole story, and tearing off a plank from the side toward the sea, he pointed out the fleet approaching, and releasing all from the prison went out with them.

But the men on the ships, having as yet heard nothing of what the army had done on the land, were completely at a loss, and slackening their sails they sent to the town of Mercurium; there they learned what had taken place at Decimum, and becoming exceedingly joyful sailed on. And when, with a favouring wind blowing, they came to within one hundred and fifty stades of Carthage, Archelaus and the soldiers bade them anchor there, fearing the warning of the general, but the sailors would not obey. For they said that the promontory at that point was without a harbour and also that the indications were that a well-known storm, which the natives call Cypriana, would arise immediately. And they predicted that, if it came upon them in that place, they would not be able to save even one of the ships. And it was as they said. So they slackened their sails for a short time and deliberated; and they did not think they ought to try for Mandracium (for they shrank from violating the commands of Belisarius, and at the same time they suspected that the entrance to Mandracium was closed by the chains, and besides they feared that this harbour was not sufficient for the whole fleet) but Stagnum seemed to them well situated (for it is forty stades distant from Carthage), and there was nothing in it to hinder them, and also it was large enough for the whole fleet. There they arrived about dusk and all anchored, except, indeed, that Calonymus with some of the sailors, disregarding the general and all the others, went off secretly to Mandracium, no one daring to hinder him, and plundered the property of the merchants dwelling on the sea, both foreigners and Carthaginians.

On the following day Belisarius commanded those on the ships to disembark, and after marshalling the whole army and drawing it up in battle formation, he marched into Carthage; for he feared lest he should encounter some snare set by the enemy. There he reminded the soldiers at length of how much good fortune had come to them because they had displayed moderation toward the Libyans, and he exhorted them earnestly to preserve good order with the greatest care in Carthage. For all the Libyans had been Romans in earlier times and had come under the Vandals by no will of their own and had suffered many outrages at the hands of these barbarians. For this very reason the emperor had entered into war with the Vandals, and it was not holy that any harm should come from them to the people whose freedom they had made the ground for taking the field against the Vandals. [Sept. 15, 533 A.D.] After such words of exhortation he entered Carthage, and, since no enemy was seen by them, he went up to the palace and seated himself on Gelimer's throne. There a crowd of merchants and other Carthaginians came before Belisarius with much shouting, persons whose homes were on the sea, and they made the charge that there had been a robbery of their property on the preceding night by the sailors. And Belisarius bound Calonymus by oaths to bring without fail all his thefts to the light. And Calonymus, taking the oath and disregarding what he had sworn, for the moment made the money his plunder, but not long afterwards he paid his just penalty in Byzantium. For being taken with the disease called apoplexy, he became insane and bit off his own tongue and then died. But this happened at a later time.

## XXI

But then, since the hour was appropriate, Belisarius commanded that lunch be prepared for them, in the very place where Gelimer was accustomed to entertain the leaders of the Vandals. This place the Romans call "Delphix," not in their own tongue, but using the Greek word according to the ancient custom. For in the palace at Rome, where the dining couches of the emperor were placed, a tripod had stood from olden times, on which the emperor's cupbearers used to place the cups. Now the Romans call a tripod "Delphix," since they were first made at Delphi, and from this both in Byzantium and wherever there is a king's dining couch they call the room "Delphix"; for the Romans follow the Greek also in calling the emperor's residence "Palatium." For a Greek named Pallas lived in this place before the capture of Troy and built a noteworthy house there, and they called this dwelling "Palatium"; and when Augustus received the imperial power, he decided to take up his first residence in that house, and from this they call the place wherever the emperor resides "Palatium." So Belisarius dined in the Delphix and with him all the notables of the army. And it happened that the lunch made for Gelimer on the preceding day was in readiness. And we feasted on that very food and the domestics of Gelimer served it and poured the wine and waited upon us in every way. And it was possible to see Fortune in her glory and making a display of the fact that all things are hers and that nothing is the private possession of any man. And it fell to the lot of Belisarius on that day to win such fame as no one of the men of his time ever won nor indeed any of the men of olden times. For though the Roman soldiers were not accustomed to enter a subject city without confusion, even if they numbered only five hundred, and especially if they made the entry unexpectedly, all the soldiers under the command of this general showed themselves so orderly that there was not a single act of insolence nor a threat, and indeed nothing happened to hinder the business of the city; but in a captured city, one which had changed its government and shifted its allegiance, it came about that no man's household was excluded from the privileges of the marketplace; on the contrary, the clerks drew up their lists of the men and conducted the soldiers to their lodgings, just as usual,[56] and the soldiers themselves, getting their lunch by purchase from the market, rested as each one wished.

Afterwards Belisarius gave pledges to those Vandals who had fled into the sanctuaries, and began to take thought for the fortifications. For the circuit-wall of Carthage had been so neglected that in many places it had become accessible to anyone who wished and easy to attack. For no small part of it had fallen down, and it was for this reason, the Carthaginians said, that Gelimer had not made his stand in the city. For he thought that it would be impossible in a short time to restore such a circuit-wall to a safe condition. And they said that an old oracle had been uttered by the children in earlier times in Carthage, to the effect that "gamma shall pursue beta, and again beta itself shall pursue gamma." And at that time it had been spoken by the children in play and had been left as an unexplained riddle, but now it was perfectly clear to all. For formerly Gizeric had driven out Boniface and now Belisarius was doing the same to Gelimer. This, then, whether it was a rumour or an oracle, came out as I have stated.

At that time a dream also came to light, which had been seen often before this by many persons, but without being clear as to how it would turn out. And the dream was as follows. Cyprian,[57] a holy man, is reverenced above all others by the Carthaginians. And they have founded a very noteworthy temple in his honour before the city on the sea-shore, in which they conduct all other customary services, and also celebrate there a festival which they call the "Cypriana"; and the sailors are accustomed to name after Cyprian the storm, which I mentioned lately,[58] giving it the same name as the festival, since it is wont to come on at the time at which the Libyans have always been accustomed to celebrate the festival. This temple the Vandals took from the Christians by violence in the reign of Honoric. And they straightway drove out their priests from the temple in great dishonour, and themselves thereafter attended to the sacred festival which, they said, now belonged to the Arians. And the Libyans, indeed, were angry on this account and altogether at a loss, but Cyprian, they say, often sent them a dream saying that there was not the least need for the Christians to be concerned about him; for he himself as time went on would be his own avenger. And when the report of this was passed around and came to all the Libyans, they were expecting that some vengeance would come upon the Vandals at some time because of this sacred festival, but were unable to conjecture how in the world the vision would be realized for them. Now, therefore, when the emperor's expedition had come to Libya, since the time had already come round and would bring the celebration of the festival on the succeeding day, the priests of the Arians, in spite of the fact that Ammatas had led the Vandals to Decimum, cleansed the whole sanctuary and were engaged in hanging up the most beautiful of the votive offerings there, and making ready the lamps and bringing out the treasures from the store-houses and preparing all things with exactness, arranging everything according to its appropriate use. But the events in Decimum turned out in the manner already described. And the priests of the Arians were off in flight, while the Christians who conform to the orthodox faith came to the temple of Cyprian, and they burned all the lamps and attended to the sacred festival just as is customary for them to perform this service, and thus it was known to all what the vision of the dream was foretelling. This, then, came about in this way.

XXII

And the Vandals, recalling an ancient saying, marvelled, understanding clearly thereafter that for a man, at least, no hope could be impossible nor any possession secure. And what this saying was and in what manner it was spoken I shall explain. When the Vandals originally, pressed by hunger, were about to remove from their ancestral abodes, a certain part of them was left behind who were reluctant to go and not desirous of following Godigisclus. And as time went on it seemed to those who had remained that they were well off as regards abundance of provisions, and Gizeric with his followers gained possession of Libya. And when this was heard by those who had not followed Godigisclus, they rejoiced, since thenceforth the country was altogether sufficient for them to live upon. But fearing lest at some time much later either the very ones who had conquered Libya, or their descendants, should in some way or other be driven out of Libya and return to their ancestral homes (for they never supposed that the Romans would let Libya be held for ever), they sent ambassadors to them. And these men, upon coming before Gizeric, said that they rejoiced with their compatriots who had met with such success, but that they were no longer able to guard the land of which he and his men had thought so little that they had settled in Libya. They prayed therefore that, if they laid no claim to their fatherland, they would bestow it as an unprofitable possession upon themselves, so that their title to the land might be made as secure as possible, and if anyone should come to do it harm, they might by no means disdain to die in behalf of it. Gizeric, accordingly, and all the other Vandals thought that they spoke fairly and justly, and they were in the act of granting everything which the envoys desired of them. But a certain old man who was esteemed among them and had a great reputation for discretion said that he would by no means permit such a thing. "For in human affairs," he said, "not one thing stands secure; nay, nothing which now exists is stable for all time for men, while as regards that which does not yet exist, there is nothing which may not come to pass." When Gizeric heard this, he expressed approval and decided to send the envoys away with nothing accomplished. Now at that time both he himself and the man who had given the advice were judged worthy of ridicule by all the Vandals, as foreseeing the impossible. But when these things which have been told took place, the Vandals learned to take a different view of the nature of human affairs and realized that the saying was that of a wise man.

Now as for those Vandals who remained in their native land, neither remembrance nor any name of them has been preserved to my time.[59] For since, I suppose, they were a small number, they were either overpowered by the neighbouring barbarians or they were mingled with them not at all unwillingly and their name gave way to that of their conquerors. Indeed, when the Vandals were conquered at that time by Belisarius, no thought occurred to them to go from there to their ancestral homes. For they were not able to convey themselves suddenly from Libya to Europe, especially as they had no ships at hand, but paid the penalty[60] there for all the wrongs they had done the Romans and especially the Zacynthians. For at one time Gizeric, falling suddenly upon the towns in the Peloponnesus, undertook to assault Taenarum. And being repulsed from there and losing many of his followers he retired in complete disorder. And while he was still filled with anger on account of this, he touched at Zacynthus, and having killed many of those he met and enslaved five hundred of the notables, he sailed away soon afterwards. And when he reached the middle of the Adriatic Sea, as it is called, he cut into small pieces the bodies of the five hundred and threw them all about the sea without the least concern. But this happened in earlier times.


XXIII

But at that time Gelimer, by distributing much money to the farmers among the Libyans and shewing great friendliness toward them, succeeded in winning many to his side. These he commanded to kill the Romans who went out into the country, proclaiming a fixed sum of gold for each man killed, to be paid to him who did the deed. And they killed many from the Roman army, not soldiers, however, but slaves and servants, who because of a desire for money went up into the villages stealthily and were caught. And the farmers brought their heads before Gelimer and departed receiving their pay, while he supposed that they had slain soldiers of the enemy.

At that time Diogenes, the aide of Belisarius, made a display of valorous deeds. For having been sent, together with twenty-two of the body-guards, to spy upon their opponents, he came to a place two days' journey distant from Carthage. And the farmers of the place, being unable to kill these men, reported to Gelimer that they were there. And he chose out and sent against them three hundred horsemen of the Vandals, enjoining upon them to bring all the men alive before him. For it seemed to him a most remarkable achievement to make captive a personal aide of Belisarius with twenty-two body-guards. Now Diogenes and his party had entered a certain house and were sleeping in the upper storey, having no thought of the enemy in mind, since, indeed, they had learned that their opponents were far away. But the Vandals, coming there at early dawn, thought it would not be to their advantage to destroy the doors of the house or to enter it in the dark, fearing lest, being involved in a night encounter, they might themselves destroy one another, and at the same time, if that should happen, provide a way of escape for a large number of the enemy in the darkness. But they did this because cowardice had paralyzed their minds, though it would have been possible for them with no trouble, by carrying torches or even without these, to catch their enemies in their beds not only without weapons, but absolutely naked besides. But as it was, they made a phalanx in a circle about the whole house and especially at the doors, and all took their stand there. But in the meantime it so happened that one of the Roman soldiers was roused from sleep, and he, noticing the noise which the Vandals made as they talked stealthily among themselves and moved with their weapons, was able to comprehend what was being done, and rousing each one of his comrades silently, he told them what was going on. And they, following the opinion of Diogenes, all put on their clothes quietly and taking up their weapons went below. There they put the bridles on their horses and leaped upon them unperceived by anyone. And after standing for a time by the court-yard entrance, they suddenly opened the door there, and straightway all came out. And then the Vandals immediately closed with them, but they accomplished nothing. For the Romans rode hard, covering themselves with their shields and warding off their assailants with their spears. And in this way Diogenes escaped the enemy, losing two of his followers, but saving the rest. He himself, however, received three blows in this encounter on the neck and the face, from which indeed he came within a little of dying, and one blow also on the left hand, as a result of which he was thereafter unable to move his little finger. This, then, took place in this way.

And Belisarius offered great sums of money to the artisans engaged in the building trade and to the general throng of workmen, and by this means he dug a trench deserving of great admiration about the circuit-wall, and setting stakes close together along it he made an excellent stockade about the fortifications. And not only this, but he built up in a short time the portions of the wall which had suffered, a thing which seemed worthy of wonder not only to the Carthaginians, but also to Gelimer himself at a later time. For when he came as a captive to Carthage, he marvelled when he saw the wall and said that his own negligence had proved the cause of all his present troubles. This, then, was accomplished by Belisarius while in Carthage.


XXIV

But Tzazon, the brother of Gelimer, reached Sardinia with the expedition which has been mentioned above[61] and disembarked at the harbour of Caranalis[62]; and at the first onset he captured the city and killed the tyrant Godas and all the fighting men about him. And when he heard that the emperor's expedition was in the land of Libya, having as yet learned nothing of what had been done there, he wrote to Gelimer as follows: "Know, O King of the Vandals and Alani, that the tyrant Godas has perished, having fallen into our hands, and that the island is again under thy kingdom, and celebrate the festival of triumph. And as for the enemy who have had the daring to march against our land, expect that their attempt will come to the same fate as that experienced by those who in former times marched against our ancestors." And those who took this letter sailed into the harbour of Carthage with no thought of the enemy in mind. And being brought by the guards before the general, they put the letter into his hands and gave him information on the matters about which he enquired, being thunderstruck at what they beheld and awed at the suddenness of the change; however, they suffered nothing unpleasant at the hand of Belisarius.

At this same time another event also occurred as follows. A short time before the emperor's expedition reached Libya, Gelimer had sent envoys into Spain, among whom were Gothaeus and Fuscias, in order to persuade Theudis, the ruler of the Visigoths,[63] to establish an alliance with the Vandals. And these envoys, upon disembarking on the mainland after crossing the strait at Gadira, found Theudis in a place situated far from the sea. And when they had come up to the place where he was, Theudis received them with friendliness and entertained them heartily, and during the feast he pretended to enquire how matters stood with Gelimer and the Vandals. Now since these envoys had travelled to him rather slowly, it happened that he had heard from others everything which had befallen the Vandals. For one merchant ship sailing for trade had put out from Carthage on the very same day as the army marched into the city, and finding a favouring wind, had come to Spain. From those on this ship Theudis learned all that had happened in Libya, but he forbade the merchants to reveal it to anyone, in order that this might not become generally known. And when Gothaeus and his followers replied that everything was as well as possible for them, he asked them for what purpose, then, they had come. And when they proposed the alliance, Theudis bade them go to the sea-coast; "For from there," he said, "you will learn of the affairs at home with certainty." And the envoys, supposing that the man was in his cups and his words were not sane, remained silent. But when on the following day they met him and made mention of the alliance, and Theudis used the same words a second time, then at length they understood that some change of fortune had befallen them in Libya, but never once thinking of Carthage they sailed for the city. And upon coming to land close by it and happening upon Roman soldiers, they put themselves in their hands to do with them as they wished. And from there they were led away to the general, and reporting the whole story, they suffered no harm at his hand. These things, then, happened thus. And Cyril,[64] upon coming near to Sardinia and learning what had happened to Godas, sailed to Carthage, and there, finding the Roman army and Belisarius victorious, he remained at rest; and Solomon[65] was sent to the emperor in order to announce what had been accomplished.


XXV

But Gelimer, upon reaching the plain of Boulla, which is distant from Carthage a journey of four days for an unencumbered traveller, not far from the boundaries of Numidia, began to gather there all the Vandals and as many of the Moors as happened to be friendly to him. Few Moors, however, joined his alliance, and these were altogether insubordinate. For all those who ruled over the Moors in Mauretania and Numidia and Byzacium sent envoys to Belisarius saying that they were slaves of the emperor and promised to fight with him. There were some also who even furnished their children as hostages and requested that the symbols of office be sent them from him according to the ancient custom. For it was a law among the Moors that no one should be a ruler over them, even if he was hostile to the Romans, until the emperor of the Romans should give him the tokens of the office. And though they had already received them from the Vandals, they did not consider that the Vandals held the office securely. Now these symbols are a staff of silver covered with gold, and a silver cap, not covering the whole head, but like a crown and held in place on all sides by bands of silver, a kind of white cloak gathered by a golden brooch on the right shoulder in the form of a Thessalian cape, and a white tunic with embroidery, and a gilded boot. And Belisarius sent these things to them, and presented each one of them with much money. However, they did not come to fight along with him, nor, on the other hand, did they dare give their support to the Vandals, but standing out of the way of both contestants, they waited to see what would be the outcome of the war. Thus, then, matters stood with the Romans.

But Gelimer sent one of the Vandals to Sardinia with a letter to his brother Tzazon. And he went quickly to the coast, and finding by chance a merchant-ship putting out to sea, he sailed into the harbour of Caranalis and put the letter into the hands of Tzazon. Now the message of the letter was as follows:

"It was not, I venture to think, Godas who caused the island to revolt from us, but some curse of madness sent from Heaven which fell upon the Vandals. For by depriving us of you and the notables of the Vandals, it has seized and carried off from the house of Gizeric absolutely all the blessings which we enjoyed. For it was not to recover the island for us that you sailed from here, but in order that Justinian might be master of Libya. For that which Fortune had decided upon previously it is now possible to know from the outcome. Belisarius, then, has come against us with a small army, but valour straightway departed and fled from the Vandals, taking good fortune with her. For Ammatas and Gibamundus have fallen, because the Vandals lost their courage, and the horses and shipyards and all Libya and, not least of all, Carthage itself, are held already by the enemy. And the Vandals are sitting here, having paid with their children and wives and all their possessions for their failure to play the part of brave men in battle, and to us is left only the plain of Boulla, where our hope in you has set us down and still keeps us. But do you have done with such matters as rebel tyrants and Sardinia and the cares concerning these things, and come to us with your whole force as quickly as possible. For when men find the very heart and centre of all in danger, it is not advisable for them to consider minutely other matters. And struggling hereafter in common against the enemy, we shall either recover our previous fortune, or gain the advantage of not bearing apart from each other the hard fate sent by Heaven."

When this letter had been brought to Tzazon, and he had disclosed its contents to the Vandals, they turned to wailing and lamentation, not openly, however, but concealing their feelings as much as possible and avoiding the notice of the islanders, silently among themselves they bewailed the fate which was upon them. And straightway setting in order matters in hand just as chance directed, they manned the ships. And sailing from there with the whole fleet, on the third day they came to land at the point of Libya which marks the boundary between the Numidians and Mauretanians. And they reached the plain of Boulla travelling on foot, and there joined with the rest of the army. And in that place there were many most pitiable scenes among the Vandals, which I, at least, could never relate as they deserve. For I think that even if one of the enemy themselves had happened to be a spectator at that time, he would probably have felt pity, in spite of himself, for the Vandals and for human fortune. For Gelimer and Tzazon threw their arms about each other's necks, and could not let go, but they spoke not a word to each other, but kept wringing their hands and weeping, and each one of the Vandals with Gelimer embraced one of those who had come from Sardinia, and did the same thing. And they stood for a long time as if grown together and found such comfort as they could in this, and neither did the men of Gelimer think fit to ask about Godas (for their present fortune had prostrated them and caused them to reckon such things as had previously seemed to them most important with those which were now utterly negligible), nor could those who came from Sardinia bring themselves to ask about what had happened in Libya. For the place was sufficient to permit them to judge of what had come to pass. And indeed they did not make any mention even of their own wives and children, knowing well that whoever of theirs was not there had either died or fallen into the hands of the enemy. Thus, then, did these things happen.

FOOTNOTES

[1] Cadiz.

[2] Sea of Azov.

[3] Abila.

[4] Or Septem Fratres.

[5] Most ancient geographers divided the inhabited world into three continents, but some made two divisions. It was a debated question with these latter whether Africa belonged to Asia or to Europe; of. Sallust, Jugurtha, 17.

[6] Kadi Keui.

[7] More correctly Hydrous, Lat. Hydruntum (Otranto).

[8] At Aulon (Avlona).

[9] Adding these four days to the other items (285, 22, 40), the total is 351 days.

[10] Calpe (Gibraltar).

[11] i.e., instead of stopping at Otranto, one might also reckon in the coast-line around the Adriatic to Dyrrachium.

[12] About twenty-four English miles.

[13] Iviza.

[14] "Black-cloaks."

[15] Belgrade.

[16] Mitrovitz.

[17] In Illyricum.

[18] He ascended the throne at the age of seven.

[19] That is, the actual occupant could enter a demurrer to the former owner's action for recovery, citing his own occupancy for thirty years or more. The new law extended the period during which the ousted proprietor could recover possession, by admitting no demurrer from the occupant so far as the years were concerned during which the Vandals should be in possession of the country.

[20] This is an error; he really ruled only eighteen months.

[21] Geiseric, Gaiseric, less properly Genseric.

[22] Now corrupted to Bona.

[23] Emperor in Gaul, Britain and Spain 383-388. Aspiring to be Emperor of the West, he invaded Italy, was defeated by Theodosius, and put to death.

[24] This is an error, for Attila died before Aetius.

[25] Including the famous treasure which Titus had brought from Jerusalem, cf. IV. ix. 5.

[26] Domitian had spent 12,000 talents (£2,400,000) on the gilding alone; Plutarch, Publ. 15.

[27] i.e. "leaders of a thousand."

[28] 130,000 Roman pounds; cf. Book I. xxii. 4. The modern equivalent is unknown.

[29] Placidia's sister, Eudocia, was wife of Honoric, Gizeric's son.

[30] See chap. iv. 27.

[31] i.e. "wisdom."

[32] Jebel Auress.

[33] i.e. to what sect or religion they belonged.

[34] Cf. Book IV. xi. 17 ff.

[35] Book I. xxii. 16.

[36] The "imperial" taxes were for the emperor's privy purse, the fiscus.

[37] These foederati were private bands of troops under the leadership of condottiere; these had the title of "count" and received from the state an allowance for the support of their bands.

[38] The medimnus equalled about one and a half bushels.

[39] i.e. "runners."

[40] Eregli, on the Sea of Marmora.

[41] Cape Matapan.

[42] Book I. xxiv. 12-15; xxv. 8-10.

[43] The ration of this twice-baked bread represented for the same weight one-fourth more wheat than when issued in the once-baked bread. He was evidently paid on the basis of so much per ration, in weight, of the once-baked bread, but on account of the length of the voyage the other kind was requisitioned.

[44] Instead of by weight.

[45] Now Porto Lombardo.

[46] Or Athalaric.

[47] Now Gozzo and Malta.

[48] Cf. III. v. 8 ff.

[49] i.e. couriers, from veredus, "post-horse."

[50] An adjutant, the general's own "choice."

[51] Topsails.

[52] i.e. Decimum miliarium, tenth milestone from Carthage.

[53] Before 533 A.D.

[54] Hermaeum, Lat. Mercurii promontorium (Cape Bon).

[55] "Auxiliaries"; see chap. xi. 3, 4.

[56] The troops were billeted as at a peaceful occupation.

[57] St. Cyprian (circa 200-257 A.D.), Bishop of Carthage.

[58] Chap. xx. 13.

[59] Compare the remarks of Gibbon, iv. p. 295.

[60] In Arcana, 18, 5 ff., Procopius estimates the number of the Vandals in Africa, at the time of Belisarius, at 80,000 males, and intimates that practically all perished.

[61] Chap. xi. 23.

[62] Cagliari.

[63] On this Theudis and his accession to the throne of the Visigoths in Spain see V. xii. 50 ff.

[64] The leader of a band of foederati. Cf. III. xi. 1, 6, xxiv. 19.

[65] Also a dux foederatorum, and domesticus of Belisarius. Cf. III. xi. 5 ff.


# Book IV: The Vandalic War (Part II)

I

Gelimer, seeing all the Vandals gathered together, led his army against Carthage. And when they came close to it, they tore down a portion of the aqueduct, a structure well worth seeing, which conducted water into the city, and after encamping for a time they withdrew, since no one of the enemy came out against them. And going about the country there they kept the roads under guard and thought that in this way they were besieging Carthage; however, they did not gather any booty, nor plunder the land, but took possession of it as their own. And at the same time they kept hoping that there would be some treason on the part of the Carthaginians themselves and such of the Roman soldiers as followed the doctrine of Arius. They also sent to the leaders of the Huns, and promising that they would have many good things from the Vandals, entreated them to become their friends and allies. Now the Huns even before this had not been well-disposed toward the cause of the Romans, since they had not indeed come to them willingly as allies (for they asserted that the Roman general Peter had given an oath and then, disregarding what had been sworn, had thus brought them to Byzantium), and accordingly they received the words of the Vandals, and promised that when they should come to real fighting they would turn with them against the Roman army. But Belisarius had a suspicion of all this (for he had heard it from the deserters), and also the circuit-wall had not as yet been completed entirely, and for these reasons he did not think it possible for his men to go out against the enemy for the present, but he was making his preparations within as well as possible. And one of the Carthaginians, Laurus by name, having been condemned on a charge of treason and proved guilty by his own secretary, was impaled by Belisarius on a hill before the city, and as a result of this the others came to feel a sort of irresistible fear and refrained from attempts at treason. And he courted the Massagetae with gifts and banquets and every other manner of flattering attention every day, and thus persuaded them to disclose to him what Gelimer had promised them on condition of their turning traitors in the battle. And these barbarians said that they had no enthusiasm for fighting, for they feared that, if the Vandals were vanquished, the Romans would not send them back to their native land, but they would be compelled to grow old and die right there in Libya; and besides they were also concerned, they said, about the booty, lest they be robbed of it. Then indeed Belisarius gave them pledges that, if the Vandals should be conquered decisively, they would be sent without the least delay to their homes with all their booty, and thus he bound them by oaths in very truth to assist the Romans with all zeal in carrying through the war.

And when all things had been prepared by him in the best way possible, and the circuit-wall had been already completed, he called together the whole army and spoke as follows: "As for exhortation, fellow Romans, I do not know that it is necessary to make any to you, men who have recently conquered the enemy so completely that Carthage here and the whole of Libya is a possession of your valour, and for this reason you will have no need of admonition that prompts to daring. For the spirits of those who have conquered are by no means wont to be overcome. But I think it not untimely to remind you of this one thing, that, if you on the present occasion but prove equal to your own selves in valour, straightway there will be an end for the Vandals of their hopes, and for you of the battle. Hence there is every reason why you should enter into this engagement with the greatest eagerness. For ever sweet to men is toil coming to an end and reaching its close. Now as for the host of the Vandals, let no one of you consider them. For not by numbers of men nor by measure of body, but by valour of soul, is war wont to be decided. And let the strongest motive which actuates men come to your minds, namely, pride in past achievement. For it is a shame, for those at least who have reason, to fall short of one's own self and to be found inferior to one's own standard of valour. For I know well that terror and the memory of misfortunes have laid hold upon the enemy and compel them to become less brave, for the one fills them with fear because of what has already happened, and the other brushes aside their hope of success. For Fortune, once seen to be bad, straightway enslaves the spirit of those who have fallen in her way. And I shall explain how the struggle involves for you at the present time a greater stake than formerly. For in the former battle the danger was, if things did not go well for us, that we should not take the land of others; but now, if we do not win the struggle, we shall lose the land which is our own. In proportion, then, as it is easier to possess nothing than to be deprived of what one has, just so now our fear touches our most vital concerns more than before. And yet formerly we had the fortune to win the victory with the infantry absent, but now, entering the battle with God propitious and with our whole army, I have hopes of capturing the camp of the enemy, men and all. Thus, then, having the end of the war ready at hand, do not by reason of any negligence put it off to another time, lest you be compelled to seek for the opportune moment after it has run past us. For when the fortune of war is postponed, its nature is not to proceed in the same manner as before, especially if the war be prolonged by the will of those who are carrying it on. For Heaven is accustomed to bring retribution always upon those who abandon the good fortune which is present. But if anyone considers that the enemy, seeing their children and wives and most precious possessions in our hands, will be daring beyond reason and will incur risks beyond the strength which they have, he does not think rightly. For an overpowering passion springing up in the heart in behalf of what is most precious is wont to diminish men's actual strength and does not allow them to make full use of their present opportunities. Considering, then, all these things, it behooves you to go with great contempt against the enemy."

II

After such words of exhortation, Belisarius sent out all the horsemen on the same day, except five hundred, and also the guardsmen and the standard, which the Romans call "bandum,"[1] entrusting them to John the Armenian, and directing him to skirmish only, if opportunity should arise. And he himself on the following day followed with the infantry forces and the five hundred horsemen. And the Massagetae, deliberating among themselves, decided, in order to seem in friendly agreement with both Gelimer and Belisarius, neither to begin fighting for the Romans nor to go over to the Vandals before the encounter, but whenever the situation of one or the other army should be bad, then to join the victors in their pursuit of the vanquished. Thus, then, had this matter been decided upon by the barbarians. And the Roman army came upon the Vandals encamped in Tricamarum, one hundred and fifty stades distant from Carthage. So they both bivouacked there at a considerable distance from one another. And when it was well on in the night, a prodigy came to pass in the Roman camp as follows. The tips of their spears were lighted with a bright fire and the points of them seemed to be burning most vigorously. This was not seen by many, but it filled with consternation the few who did see it, not knowing how it would come out. And this happened to the Romans in Italy again at a much later time. And at that time, since they knew by experience, they believed it to be a sign of victory. But now, as I have said, since this was the first time it had happened, they were filled with consternation and passed the night in great fear.

And on the following day Gelimer commanded the Vandals to place the women and children and all their possessions in the middle of the stockade, although it had not the character of a fort, and calling all together, he spoke as follows: "It is not to gain glory, or to retrieve the loss of empire alone, O fellow Vandals, that we are about to fight, so that even if we wilfully played the coward and sacrificed these our belongings we might possibly live, sitting at home and keeping our own possessions; but you see, surely, that our fortunes have come round to such a pass that, if we do not gain the mastery over the enemy, we shall, if we perish, leave them as masters of these our children and our wives and our land and all our possessions, while if we survive, there will be added our own enslavement and to behold all these enslaved; but if, indeed, we overcome our foes in the war, we shall, if we live, pass our lives among all good things, or, after the glorious ending of our lives, there will be left to our wives and children the blessings of prosperity, while the name of the Vandals will survive and their empire be preserved. For if it has ever happened to any men to be engaged in a struggle for their all, we now more than all others realize that we are entering the battle-line with our hopes for all we have resting wholly upon ourselves. Not for our bodies, then, is our fear, nor in death is our danger, but in being defeated by the enemy. For if we lose the victory, death will be to our advantage. Since, therefore, the case stands so, let no one of the Vandals weaken, but let him proudly expose his body, and from shame at the evils that follow defeat let him court the end of life. For when a man is ashamed of that which is shameful, there is always present with him a dauntless courage in the face of danger. And let no recollection of the earlier battle come into your minds. For it was not by cowardice on our part that we were defeated, but we tripped upon obstacles interposed by fortune and were overthrown. Now it is not the way of the tide of fortune to flow always in the same direction, but every day, as a rule, it is wont to change about. In manliness it is our boast that we surpass the enemy, and that in numbers we are much superior; for we believe that we surpass them no less than tenfold. And why shall I add that many and great are the incentives which, now especially, urge us on to valour, naming the glory of our ancestors and the empire which has been handed down to us by them? For in our case that glory is obscured by our unlikeness to our kindred, while the empire is bent upon fleeing from us as unworthy. And I pass over in silence the wails of these poor women and the tears of our children, by which, as you see, I am now so deeply moved that I am unable to prolong my discourse. But having said this one thing, I shall stop, that there will be for us no returning to these most precious possessions if we do not gain the mastery over the enemy. Remembering these things, shew yourselves brave men and do not bring shame upon the fame of Gizeric."

After speaking such words, Gelimer commanded his brother Tzazon to deliver an exhortation separately to the Vandals who had come with him from Sardinia. And he gathered them together a little apart from the camp and spoke as follows: "For all the Vandals, fellow soldiers, the struggle is in behalf of those things which you have just heard the king recount, but for you, in addition to all the other considerations, it so happens that you are vying with yourselves. For you have recently been victorious in a struggle for the maintenance of our rule, and you have recovered the island for the empire of the Vandals; there is every reason, therefore, for you to make still greater display of your valour. For those whose hazard involves the greatest things must needs display the greatest zeal for warfare also. Indeed, when men who struggle for the maintenance of their rule are defeated, should it so happen, they have not failed in the most vital part; but when men are engaged in battle for their all, surely their very lives are influenced by the outcome of the struggle. And for the rest, if you shew yourselves brave men at the present time, you will thereby prove with certainty that the destruction[2] of the tyrant Godas was an achievement of valour on your part; but if you weaken now, you will be deprived of even the renown of those deeds, as of something which does not belong to you at all. And yet, even apart from this, it is reasonable to think that you will have an advantage over the rest of the Vandals in this battle. For those who have failed are dismayed by their previous fortune, while those who have encountered no reverse enter the struggle with their courage unimpaired. And this too, I think, will not be spoken out of season, that if we conquer the enemy, it will be you who will win the credit for the greatest part of the victory, and all will call you saviours of the nation of the Vandals. For men who achieve renown in company with those who have previously met with misfortune naturally claim the better fortune as their own. Considering all these things, therefore, I say that you should bid the women and children who are lamenting their fate to take courage even now, should summon God to fight with us, should go with enthusiasm against the enemy, and lead the way for our compatriots into this battle."


III

After both Gelimer and Tzazon had spoken such exhortations, they led out the Vandals, and at about the time of lunch, when the Romans were not expecting them, but were preparing their meal, they were at hand and arrayed themselves for battle along the bank of the stream. Now the stream at that place is an ever-flowing one, to be sure, but its volume is so small that it is not even given a special name by the inhabitants of the place, but it is designated simply as a brook. So the Romans came to the other bank of this river, after preparing themselves as well as they could under the circumstances, and arrayed themselves as follows. The left wing was held by Martinus and Valerian, John, Cyprian, Althias, and Marcellus, and as many others as were commanders of the foederati[3]; and the right was held by Pappas, Barbatus, and Aïgan, and the others who commanded the forces of cavalry. And in the centre John took his position, leading the guards and spearmen of Belisarius and carrying the general's standard. And Belisarius also came there at the opportune moment with his five hundred horsemen, leaving the infantry behind advancing at a walk. For all the Huns had been arrayed in another place, it being customary for them even before this not to mingle with the Roman army if they could avoid so doing, and at that time especially, since they had in mind the purpose which has previously been explained,[4] it was not their wish to be arrayed with the rest of the army. Such, then, was the formation of the Romans. And on the side of the Vandals, either wing was held by the chiliarchs, and each one led the division under him, while in the centre was Tzazon, the brother of Gelimer, and behind him were arrayed the Moors. But Gelimer himself was going about everywhere exhorting them and urging them on to daring. And the command had been previously given to all the Vandals to use neither spear nor any other weapon in this engagement except their swords.

After a considerable time had passed and no one began the battle, John chose out a few of those under him by the advice of Belisarius and crossing the river made an attack on the centre, where Tzazon crowded them back and gave chase. And the Romans in flight came into their own camp, while the Vandals in pursuit came as far as the stream, but did not cross it. And once more John, leading out more of the guardsmen of Belisarius, made a dash against the forces of Tzazon, and again being repulsed from there, withdrew to the Roman camp. And a third time with almost all the guards and spearmen of Belisarius he took the general's standard and made his attack with much shouting and a great noise. But since the barbarians manfully withstood them and used only their swords, the battle became fierce, and many of the noblest of the Vandals fell, and among them Tzazon himself, the brother of Gelimer. Then at last the whole Roman army was set in motion, and crossing the river they advanced upon the enemy, and the rout, beginning at the centre, became complete; for each of the Roman divisions turned to flight those before them with no trouble. And the Massagetae, seeing this, according to their agreement among themselves[5] joined the Roman army in making the pursuit, but this pursuit was not continued for a great distance. For the Vandals entered their own camp quickly and remained quiet, while the Romans, thinking that they would not be able to fight it out with them inside the stockade, stripped such of the corpses as had gold upon them and retired to their own camp. And there perished in this battle, of the Romans less than fifty, but of the Vandals about eight hundred.

But Belisarius, when the infantry came up in the late afternoon, moved as quickly as he could with the whole army and went against the camp of the Vandals. And Gelimer, realising that Belisarius with his infantry and the rest of his army was coming against him straightway, without saying a word or giving a command leaped upon his horse and was off in flight on the road leading to Numidia. And his kinsmen and some few of his domestics followed him in utter consternation and guarding with silence what was taking place. And for some time it escaped the notice of the Vandals that Gelimer had run away, but when they all perceived that he had fled, and the enemy were already plainly seen, then indeed the men began to shout and the children cried out and the women wailed. And they neither took with them the money they had nor did they heed the laments of those dearest to them, but every man fled in complete disorder just as he could. And the Romans, coming up, captured the camp, money and all, with not a man in it; and they pursued the fugitives throughout the whole night, killing all the men upon whom they happened, and making slaves of the women and children. And they found in this camp a quantity of wealth such as has never before been found, at least in one place. For the Vandals had plundered the Roman domain for a long time and had transferred great amounts of money to Libya, and since their land was an especially good one, nourishing abundantly with the most useful crops, it came about that the revenue collected from the commodities produced there was not paid out to any other country in the purchase of a food supply, but those who possessed the land always kept for themselves the income from it for the ninety-five years during which the Vandals ruled Libya. And from this it resulted that their wealth, amounting to an extraordinary sum, returned once more on that day into the hands of the Romans. So this battle and the pursuit and the capture of the Vandals' camp happened three months after the Roman army came to Carthage, at about the middle of the last month, which the Romans call "December." [533 A.D.]


IV


Then Belisarius, seeing the Roman army rushing about in confusion and great disorder, was disturbed, being fearful throughout the whole night lest the enemy, uniting by mutual agreement against him, should do him irreparable harm. And if this thing had happened at that time in any way at all, I believe that, not one of the Romans would have escaped and enjoyed this booty. For the soldiers, being extremely poor men, upon becoming all of a sudden masters of very great wealth and of women both young and extremely comely, were no longer able to restrain their minds or to find any satiety in the things they had, but were so intoxicated, drenched as they were by their present good fortunes, that each one wished to take everything with him back to Carthage. And they were going about, not in companies but alone or by twos, wherever hope led them, searching out everything roundabout among the valleys and the rough country and wherever there chanced to be a cave or anything such as might bring them into danger or ambush. For neither did fear of the enemy nor their respect for Belisarius occur to them, nor indeed anything else at all except the desire for spoils, and being overmastered by this they came to think lightly of everything else. And Belisarius, taking note of all this, was at a loss as to how he should handle the situation. But at daybreak he took his stand upon a certain hill near the road, appealing to the discipline which no longer existed and heaping reproaches upon all, soldiers and officers alike. Then indeed, those who chanced to be near, and especially those who were of the household of Belisarius, sent the money and slaves which they had to Carthage with their tentmates and messmates, and themselves came up beside the general and gave heed to the orders given them.

And he commanded John, the Armenian, with two hundred men to follow Gelimer, and without slackening their speed either night or day to pursue him, until they should take him living or dead. And he sent word to his associates in Carthage to lead into the city all the Vandals who were sitting as suppliants in sanctuaries in the places about the city, giving them pledges and taking away their weapons, that they might not begin an uprising, and to keep them there until he himself should come. And with those who were left he went about everywhere and gathered the soldiers hastily, and to all the Vandals he came upon he gave pledges for their safety. For it was no longer possible to catch anyone of the Vandals except as a suppliant in the sanctuaries. And from these he took away their weapons and sent them, with soldiers to guard them, to Carthage, not giving them time to unite against the Romans. And when everything was as well settled as possible, he himself with the greater part of the army moved against Gelimer with all speed. But John, after continuing the pursuit five days and nights, had already come not far from Gelimer, and in fact he was about to engage with him on the following day. But since it was not fated that Gelimer should be captured by John, the following obstacle was contrived by fortune. Among those pursuing with John it happened that there was Uliaris, the aide of Belisarius. Now this man was a passionate fellow and well favoured in strength of heart and body, but not a very serious man, but one who generally took delight in wine and buffoonery. This Uliaris on the sixth day of the pursuit, being drunk, saw a bird sitting in a tree at about sunrise, and he quickly stretched his bow and despatched a missile at the bird. And he missed the bird, but John, who was behind it, he hit in the neck by no will of his own. And since the wound was mortal, John passed away a short time afterwards, leaving great sorrow at his loss to the Emperor Justinian and Belisarius, the general, and to all the Romans and Carthaginians. For in manliness and every sort of virtue he was well endowed, and he shewed himself, to those who associated with him, gentle and equitable to a degree quite unsurpassed. Thus, then, John fulfilled his destiny. As for Uliaris, when he came to himself, he fled to a certain village which was near by and sat as a suppliant in the sanctuary there. And the soldiers no longer pressed the pursuit of Gelimer, but they cared for John as long as he survived, and when he had died they carried out all the customary rites in his burial, and reporting the whole matter to Belisarius they remained where they were. And as soon as he heard of it, he came to John's burial, and bewailed his fate. And after weeping over him and grieving bitterly at the whole occurrence, he honoured the tomb of John with many gifts and especially by providing for it a regular income. However, he did nothing severe to Uliaris, since the soldiers said that John had enjoined upon them by the most dread oaths that no vengeance should come to him, since he had not performed the unholy deed with deliberate intent.

Thus, then, Gelimer escaped falling into the hands of the enemy on that day. And from that time on Belisarius pursued him, but upon reaching a strong city of Numidia situated on the sea, ten days distant from Carthage, which they call Hippo Regius,[6] he learned that Gelimer had ascended the mountain Papua and could no longer be captured by the Romans. Now this mountain is situated at the extremity of Numidia and is exceedingly precipitous and climbed only with the greatest difficulty (for lofty cliffs rise up toward it from every side), and on it dwell barbarian Moors, who were friends and allies to Gelimer, and an ancient city named Medeus lies on the outskirts of the mountain. There Gelimer rested with his followers. But as for Belisarius, he was not able to make any attempt at all on the mountain, much less in the winter season, and since his affairs were still in an uncertain state, he did not think it advisable to be away from Carthage; and so he chose out soldiers, with Pharas as their leader, and set them to maintain the siege of the mountain. Now this Pharas was energetic and thoroughly serious and upright in every way, although he was an Erulian by birth. And for an Erulian not to give himself over to treachery and drunkenness, but to strive after uprightness, is no easy matter and merits abundant praise.[7] But not only was it Pharas who maintained orderly conduct, but also all the Erulians who followed him. This Pharas, then, Belisarius commanded to establish himself at the foot of the mountain during the winter season and to keep close guard, so that it would neither be possible for Gelimer to leave the mountain nor for any supplies to be brought in to him. And Pharas acted accordingly. Then Belisarius turned to the Vandals who were sitting as suppliants in the sanctuaries in Hippo Regius, and there were many of them and of the nobility, and he caused them all to accept pledges and arise, and then he sent them to Carthage with a guard. And there it came about that the following event happened to him.

In the house of Gelimer there was a certain scribe named Boniface, a Libyan, and a native of Byzacium, a man exceedingly faithful to Gelimer. At the beginning of this war Gelimer had put this Boniface on a very swift-sailing ship, and placing all the royal treasure in it commanded him to anchor in the harbour of Hippo Regius, and if he should see that the situation was not favourable to their side, he was to sail with all speed to Spain with the money, and go to Theudis, the leader of the Visigoths, where he was expecting to find safety for himself also, should the fortune of war prove adverse for the Vandals. So Boniface, as long as he felt hope for the cause of the Vandals, remained there; but as soon as the battle in Tricamarum took place, with all the other events which have been related, he spread his canvas and sailed away just as Gelimer had directed him. But an opposing wind brought him back, much against his will, into the harbour of Hippo Regius. And since he had already heard that the enemy were somewhere near, he entreated the sailors with many promises to row with all their might for some other continent or for an island. But they were unable to do so, since a very severe storm had fallen upon them and the waves of the sea were rising to a great height, seeing that it was the Tuscan sea,[8] and then it occurred to them and to Boniface that, after all, God wished to give the money to the Romans and so was not allowing the ship to put out. However, though they had got outside the harbour, they encountered great danger in bringing their ship back to anchorage. And when Belisarius arrived at Hippo Regius, Boniface sent some men to him. These he commanded to sit in a sanctuary, and they were to say that they had been sent by Boniface, who had the money of Gelimer, but to conceal the place where he was, until they should receive the pledges of Belisarius that upon giving Gelimer's money he himself should escape free from harm, having all that was his own. These men, then, acted according to these instructions, and Belisarius was pleased at the good news and did not decline to take an oath. And sending some of his associates he took the treasure of Gelimer and released Boniface in possession of his own money and also with an enormous sum which he plundered from Gelimer's treasure.


V


And when he returned to Carthage, he put all the Vandals in readiness, so that at the opening of spring he might send them to Byzantium; and he sent out an army to recover for the Romans everything which the Vandals ruled. And first he sent Cyril to Sardinia with a great force, having the head of Tzazon, since these islanders were not at all willing to yield to the Romans, fearing the

Vandals and thinking that what had been told them as having happened in Tricamarum could not be true. And he ordered this Cyril to send a portion of the army to Corsica, and to recover for the Roman empire the island, which had been previously subject to the Vandals; this island was called Cyrnus in early times, and is not far from Sardinia. So he came to Sardinia and displayed the head of Tzazon to the inhabitants of the place, and he won back both the islands and made them tributary to the Roman domain. And to Caesarea[9] in Mauretania Belisarius sent John with an infantry company which he usually commanded himself; this place is distant from Carthage a journey of thirty days for an unencumbered traveller, as one goes towards Gadira and the west; and it is situated upon the sea, having been a great and populous city from ancient times. Another John, one of his own guardsmen, he sent to Gadira on the strait and by one of the Pillars of Heracles, to take possession of the fort there which they call "Septem."[10] And to the islands which are near the strait where the ocean flows in, called Ebusa and Majorica and Minorica[11] by the natives, he sent Apollinarius, who was a native of Italy, but had come while still a lad to Libya. And he had been rewarded with great sums of money by Ilderic, who was then leader of the Vandals, and after Ilderic had been removed from the office and was in confinement, as has been told in the previous narrative,[12] he came to the Emperor Justinian with the other Libyans who were working in the interest of Ilderic, in order to entreat his favour as a suppliant. And he joined the Roman expedition against Gelimer and the Vandals, and proved himself a brave man in this war and most of all at Tricamarum. And as a result of his deeds there Belisarius entrusted to him these islands. And later Belisarius sent an army also into Tripolis to Pudentius and Tattimuth,[13] who were being pressed by the Moors there, and thus strengthened the Roman power in that quarter.

He also sent some men to Sicily in order to take the fortress in Lilybaeum, as belonging to the Vandals' kingdom,[14] but he was repulsed from there, since the Goths by no means saw fit to yield any part of Sicily, on the ground that this fortress did not belong to the Vandals at all. And when Belisarius heard this, he wrote to the commanders who were there as follows: "You are depriving us of Lilybaeum, the fortress of the Vandals who are the slaves of the emperor, and are not acting justly nor in a way to benefit yourselves, and you wish to bring upon your ruler, though he does not so will it and is far distant from the scene of these actions, the hostility of the great emperor, whose good-will he has, having won it with great labour. And yet how could you but seem to be acting contrary to the ways of men, it you recently allowed Gelimer to hold the fortress, but have decided to wrest from the emperor, Gelimer's master, the possessions of the slave? You, at least, should not act thus, most excellent sirs. But reflect that, while it is the nature of friendship to cover over many faults, hostility does not brook even the smallest misdeeds, but searches the past for every offence, and allows not its enemy to grow rich on what does not in the least belong to them.[15] Moreover, the enemy fights to avenge the wrongs which it says have been done to its ancestors; and whereas, if friendship thus turned to hostility fails in the struggle, it suffers no loss of its own possessions, yet if it succeeds, it teaches the vanquished to take a new view of the indulgence which has been shewn them in the past. See to it, then, that you neither do us further harm nor suffer harm yourselves, and do not make the great emperor an enemy to the Gothic nation, when it is your prayer that he be propitious toward you. For be well assured that, if you lay claim to this fortress, war will confront you immediately, and not for Lilybaeum alone, but for all the possessions you claim as yours, though not one of them belongs to you."

Such was the message of the letter. And the Goths reported these things to the mother[16] of Antalaric, and at her direction made the following reply: "The letter which you have written, most excellent Belisarius, carries sound admonition, but pertinent to some other men, not to us the Goths. For there is nothing of the Emperor Justinian's which we have taken and hold; may we never be so mad as to do such a thing! The whole of Sicily we claim because it is our own, and the fortress of Lilybaeum is one of its promontories. And if Theoderic gave his sister, who was the consort of the king of the Vandals, one of the trading-ports of Sicily for her use, this is nothing. For this fact could not afford a basis for any claim on your part. But you, O General, would be acting justly toward us, if you should be willing to make the settlement of the matters in dispute between us, not as an enemy, but as a friend. And there is this difference, that friends are accustomed to settle their disagreements by arbitration, but enemies by battle. We, therefore, shall commit this matter to the Emperor Justinian, to arbitrate[17] in whatever manner seems to him lawful and just. And we desire that the decisions you make shall be as wise as possible, rather than as hasty as possible, and that you, therefore, await the decision of your emperor." Such was the message of the letter of the Goths. And Belisarius, reporting all to the emperor, remained quiet until the emperor should send him word what his wish was.


VI

But Pharas, having by this time become weary of the siege for many reasons, and especially because of the winter season, and at the same time thinking that the Moors there would not be able to stand in his way, undertook the ascent of Papua with great zeal. Accordingly he armed all his followers very carefully and began the ascent. But the Moors rushed to the defence, and since they were on ground which was steep and very hard to traverse, their efforts to hinder those making the ascent were easily accomplished. But Pharas fought hard to force the ascent, and one hundred and ten of his men perished in this struggle, and he himself with the remainder was beaten back and retired; and as a result of this he did not dare to attempt the ascent again, since the situation was against him, but he established as careful a guard as possible, in order that those on Papua, being pressed by hunger, might surrender themselves; and he neither permitted them to run away nor anything to be brought in to them from outside. Then, indeed, it came about that Gelimer and those about him, who were nephews and cousins of his and other persons of high birth, experienced a misery which no one could describe, however eloquent he might be, in a way which would equal the facts. For of all the nations which we know that of the Vandals is the most luxurious, and that of the Moors the most hardy. For the Vandals, since the time when they gained possession of Libya, used to indulge in baths, all of them, every day, and enjoyed a table abounding in all things, the sweetest and best that the earth and sea produce. And they wore gold very generally, and clothed themselves in the Medic garments, which now they call "seric,"[18] and passed their time, thus dressed, in theatres and hippodromes and in other pleasureable pursuits, and above all else in hunting. And they had dancers and mimes and all other things to hear and see which are of a musical nature or otherwise merit attention among men. And the most of them dwelt in parks, which were well supplied with water and trees; and they had great numbers of banquets, and all manner of sexual pleasures were in great vogue among them. But the Moors live in stuffy huts[19] both in winter and in summer and at every other time, never removing from them either because of snow or the heat of the sun or any other discomfort whatever due to nature. And they sleep on the ground, the prosperous among them, if it should so happen, spreading a fleece under themselves. Moreover, it is not customary among them to change their clothing with the seasons, but they wear a thick cloak and a rough shirt at all times. And they have neither bread nor wine nor any other good thing, but they take grain, either wheat or barley, and, without boiling it or grinding it to flour or barley-meal, they eat it in a manner not a whit different from that of animals. Since the Moors, then, were of a such a sort, the followers of Gelimer, after living with them for a long time and changing their accustomed manner of life to such a miserable existence, when at last even the necessities of life had failed, held out no longer, but death was thought by them most sweet and slavery by no means disgraceful.

Now when this was learned by Pharas, he wrote to Gelimer as follows: "I too am a barbarian and not accustomed to writing and speaking, nor am I skilful in these matters. But that which I am forced as a man to know, having learned from the nature of things, this I am writing you. What in the world has happened to you, my dear Gelimer, that you have cast, not yourself alone, but your whole family besides, into this pit? Is it, forsooth, that you may avoid becoming a slave? But this is assuredly nothing but youthful folly, and making of 'liberty' a mere shibboleth, as though liberty were worth possessing at the price of all this misery! And, after all, do you not consider that you are, even now, a slave to the most wretched of the Moors, since your only hope of being saved, if the best happens, is in them? And yet why would it not be better in every way to be a slave among the Romans and beggared, than to be monarch on Mount Papua with Moors as your subjects? But of course it seems to you the very height of disgrace even to be a fellow slave with Belisarius! Away with the thought, most excellent Gelimer. Are not we,[20] who also are born of noble families, proud that we are now in the service of an emperor? And indeed they say that it is the wish of the Emperor Justinian to have you enrolled in the senate, thus sharing in the highest honour and being a patrician, as we term that rank, and to present you with lands both spacious and good and with great sums of money, and that Belisarius is willing to make himself responsible for your having all these things, and to give you pledges. Now as for all the miseries which fortune has brought you, you are able to bear with fortitude whatever comes from her, knowing that you are but a man and that these things are inevitable; but if fortune has purposed to temper these adversities with some admixture of good, would you of yourself refuse to accept this gladly? Or should we consider that the good gifts of fortune are not just as inevitable as are her undesirable gifts? Yet such is not the opinion of even the utterly senseless; but you, it would seem, have now lost your good judgment, steeped as you are in misfortunes. Indeed, discouragement is wont to confound the mind and to be transformed to folly. If, however, you can bear your own thoughts and refrain from rebelling against fortune when she changes, it will be possible at this very moment for you to choose that which will be wholly to your advantage, and to escape from the evils which hang over you."

When Gelimer had read this letter and wept bitterly over it, he wrote in reply as follows: "I am both deeply grateful to you for the advice which you have given me and I also think it unbearable to be a slave to an enemy who wrongs me, from whom I should pray God to exact justice, if He should be propitious to me, an enemy who, though he had never experienced any harm from me either in deeds which he suffered or in words which he heard, provided a pretext for a war which was unprovoked, and reduced me to this state of misfortune, bringing Belisarius against me from I know not where. And yet it is not at all unlikely that he also, since he is but a man, though he be emperor too, may have something befall him which he would not choose. But as for me, I am not able to write further. For my present misfortune has robbed me of my thoughts. Farewell, then, dear Pharas, and send me a lyre and one loaf of bread and a sponge, I pray you." When this reply was read by Pharas, he was at a loss for some time, being unable to understand the final words of the letter, until he who had brought the letter explained that Gelimer desired one loaf because he was eager to enjoy the sight of it and to eat it, since from the time when he went up upon Papua he had not seen a single baked loaf. A sponge also was necessary for him; for one of his eyes, becoming irritated by lack of washing, was greatly swollen. And being a skilful harpist he had composed an ode relating to his present misfortune, which he was eager to chant to the accompaniment of a lyre while he wept out his soul. When Pharas heard this, he was deeply moved, and lamenting the fortune of men, he did as was written and sent all the things which Gelimer desired of him. However he relaxed the siege not a whit, but kept watch more closely than before.


VII

And already a space of three months had been spent in this siege and the winter was coming to an end. And Gelimer was afraid, suspecting that his besiegers would come up against him after no great time; and the bodies of most of the children who were related to him[21] were discharging worms in this time of misery. And though in everything he was deeply distressed, and looked upon everything, except, indeed, death, with dissatisfaction, he nevertheless endured the suffering beyond all expectation, until it happened that he beheld a sight such as the following. A certain Moorish woman had managed somehow to crush a little corn, and making of it a very tiny cake, threw it into the hot ashes on the hearth. For thus it is the custom among the Moors to bake their loaves. And beside this hearth two children were sitting, in exceedingly great distress by reason of their hunger, the one being the son of the very woman who had thrown in the cake, and the other a nephew of Gelimer; and they were eager to seize the cake as soon as it should seem to them to be cooked. And of the two children the Vandal got ahead of the other and snatched the cake first, and, though it was still exceedingly hot and covered with ashes, hunger overpowered him, and he threw it into his mouth and was eating it, when the other seized him by the hair of the head and struck him over the temple and beat him again and thus compelled him with great violence to cast out the cake which was already in his throat. This sad experience Gelimer could not endure (for he had followed all from the beginning), and his spirit was weakened and he wrote as quickly as possible to Pharas as follows: "If it has ever happened to any man, after manfully enduring terrible misfortunes, to take a course contrary to that which he had previously determined upon, consider me to be such a one, O most excellent Pharas. For there has come to my mind your advice, which I am far from wishing to disregard. For I cannot resist fortune further nor rebel against fate, but I shall follow straightway wherever it seems to her best to lead; but let me receive the pledges, that Belisarius guarantees that the emperor will do everything which you recently promised me. For I, indeed, as soon as you give the pledges, shall put both myself into your hands and these kinsmen of mine and the Vandals, as many as are here with us."

Such were the words written by Gelimer in this letter. And Pharas, having signified this to Belisarius, as well as what they had previously written to each other, begged him to declare as quickly as possible what his wish was. And Belisarius (since he was greatly desirous of leading Gelimer alive to the emperor), as soon as he had read the letter, became overjoyed and commanded Cyprian, a leader of foederati,[22] to go to Papua with certain others, and directed them to give an oath concerning the safety of Gelimer and of those with him, and to swear that he would be honoured before the emperor and would lack nothing. And when these men had come to Pharas, they went with him to a certain place by the foot of the mountain, where Gelimer came at their summons, and after receiving the pledges just as he wished he came with them to Carthage. And it happened that Belisarius was staying for a time in the suburb of the city which they call Aclas. Accordingly Gelimer came before him in that place, laughing with such laughter as was neither moderate nor the kind one could conceal, and some of those who were looking at him suspected that by reason of the extremity of his affliction he had changed entirely from his natural state and that, already beside himself, he was laughing for no reason. But his friends would have it that the man was in his sound mind, and that because he had been born in a royal family, and had ascended the throne, and had been clothed with great power and immense wealth from childhood even to old age, and then being driven to flight and plunged into great fear had undergone the sufferings on Papua, and now had come as a captive, having in this way had experience of all the gifts of fortune, both good and evil, for this reason, they believed, he thought that man's lot was worthy of nothing else than much laughter. Now concerning this laughter of Gelimer's, let each one speak according to his judgment, both enemy and friend. But Belisarius, reporting to the emperor that Gelimer was a captive in Carthage, asked permission to bring him to Byzantium with him. At the same time he guarded both him and all the Vandals in no dishonour and proceeded to put the fleet in readiness.

Now many other things too great to be hoped for have before now been experienced in the long course of time, and they will continue as long as the fortunes of men are the same as they now are; for those things which seem to reason impossible are actually accomplished, and many times those things which previously appeared impossible, when they have befallen, have seemed to be worthy of wonder; but whether such events as these ever took place before I am not able to say, wherein the fourth descendant of Gizeric, and his kingdom at the height of its wealth and military strength, were completely undone in so short a time by five thousand men coming in as invaders and having not a place to cast anchor. For such was the number of the horsemen who followed Belisarius, and carried through the whole war against the Vandals. For whether this happened by chance or because of some kind of valour, one would justly marvel at it. But I shall return to the point from which I have strayed.

VIII

So the Vandalic war ended thus. But envy, as is wont to happen in cases of great good fortune, was already swelling against Belisarius, although he provided no pretext for it. For some of the officers slandered him to the emperor, charging him, without any grounds whatever, with seeking to set up a kingdom for himself,[23] a statement for which there was no basis whatever. But the emperor did not disclose these things to the world, either because he paid no heed to the slander, or because this course seemed better to him. But he sent Solomon and gave Belisarius the opportunity to choose whichever of two things he desired, either to come to Byzantium with Gelimer and the Vandals, or to remain there and send them. And Belisarius, since it did not escape him that the officers were bringing against him the charge of seeking supreme power, was eager to get to Byzantium, in order that he might clear himself of the charge and be able to proceed against his slanderers. Now as to the manner in which he learned of the attempt of his accusers, I shall explain. When those who denounced him wished to present this slander, fearing lest the man who was to carry their letter to the emperor should be lost at sea and thus put a stop to their proceedings, they wrote the aforesaid accusation on two tablets, purposing to send two messengers to the emperor in two ships. And one of these two sailed away without being detected, but the second, on account of some suspicion or other, was captured in Mandracium, and putting the writing into the hands of his captors, he made known what was being done. So Belisarius, having learned in this way, was eager to come before the emperor, as has been said. Such, then, was the course of these events at Carthage.

But the Moors who dwelt in Byzacium and in Numidia turned to revolt for no good reason, and they decided to break the treaty and to rise suddenly against the Romans. And this was not out of keeping with their peculiar character. For there is among the Moors neither fear of God nor respect for men. For they care not either for oaths or for hostages, even though the hostages chance to be the children or brothers of their leaders. Nor is peace maintained among the Moors by any other means than by fear of the enemies opposing them. Now I shall set forth in what manner the treaty was made by them with Belisarius and how it was broken. When it came to be expected that the emperor's expedition would arrive in Libya, the Moors, fearing lest they should receive some harm from it, consulted the oracles of their women. For it is not lawful in this nation for a man to utter oracles, but the women among them as a result of some sacred rites become possessed and foretell the future, no less than any of the ancient oracles. So on that occasion, when they made enquiry, as has been said, the women gave the response: "There shall be a host from the waters, the overthrow of the Vandals, destruction and defeat of the Moors, when the general of the Romans shall come unbearded." When the Moors heard this, since they saw that the emperor's army had come from the sea, they began to be in great fear and were quite unwilling to fight in alliance with the Vandals, but they sent to Belisarius and established peace, as has been stated previously,[24] and then remained quiet and waited for the future, to see how it would fall out. And when the power of the Vandals had now come to an end, they sent to the Roman army, investigating whether there was anyone unbearded among them holding an office. And when they saw all wearing full beards, they thought that the oracle did not indicate the present time to them, but one many generations later, interpreting the saying in that way which they themselves wished. Immediately, therefore, they were eager to break the treaty, but their fear of Belisarius prevented them. For they had no hope that they would ever overcome the Romans in war, at least with him present. But when they heard that he was making his departure together with his guards and spearmen, and that the ships were already being filled with them and the Vandals, they suddenly rose in arms and displayed every manner of outrage upon the Libyans. For the soldiers were both few in each place on the frontier and still unprepared, so that they would not have been able to stand against the barbarians as they made inroads at every point, nor to prevent their incursions, which took place frequently and not in an open manner. But men were being killed indiscriminately and women with their children were being made slaves, and the wealth was being plundered from every part of the frontier and the whole country was being filled with fugitives. These things were reported to Belisarius when he was just about setting sail. And since it was now too late for him to return himself, he entrusted Solomon with the administration of Libya and he also chose out the greatest part of his own guards and spearmen, instructing them to follow Solomon and as quickly as possible to punish with all zeal those of the Moors who had risen in revolt and to exact vengeance for the injury done the Romans. And the emperor sent another army also to Solomon with Theodoras, the Cappadocian, and Ildiger, who was the son-in-law of Antonina, the wife of Belisarius. And since it was no longer possible to find the revenues of the districts of Libya set down in order in documents, as the Romans had recorded them in former times,[25] inasmuch as Gizeric had upset and destroyed everything in the beginning, Tryphon and Eustratius were sent by the emperor, in order to assess the taxes for the Libyans each according to his proportion. But these men seemed to the Libyans neither moderate nor endurable.

IX

Belisarius, upon reaching Byzantium with Gelimer and the Vandals, was counted worthy to receive such honours, as in former times were assigned to those generals of the Romans who had won the greatest and most noteworthy victories. And a period of about six hundred years had now passed since anyone had attained these honours,[26] except, indeed, Titus and Trajan, and such other emperors as had led armies against some barbarian nation and had been victorious. For he displayed the spoils and slaves from the war in the midst of the city and led a procession which the Romans call a "triumph," not, however, in the ancient manner, but going on foot from his own house to the hippodrome and then again from the barriers until he reached the place where the imperial throne is.[27] And there was booty, first of all, whatever articles are wont to be set apart for the royal service, thrones of gold and carriages in which it is customary for a king's consort to ride, and much jewelry made of precious stones, and golden drinking cups, and all the other things which are useful for the royal table. And there was also silver weighing many thousands of talents and all the royal treasure amounting to an exceedingly great sum (for Gizeric had despoiled the Palatium in Rome, as has been said in the preceding narrative),[28] and among these were the treasures of the Jews, which Titus, the son of Vespasian, together with certain others, had brought to Rome after the capture of Jerusalem. And one of the Jews, seeing these things, approached one of those known to the emperor and said: "These treasures I think it inexpedient to carry into the palace in Byzantium. Indeed, it is not possible for them to be elsewhere than in the place where Solomon, the king of the Jews, formerly placed them. For it is because of these that Gizeric captured the palace of the Romans, and that now the Roman army has captured that the Vandals." When this had been brought to the ears of the Emperor, he became afraid and quickly sent everything to the sanctuaries of the Christians in Jerusalem. And there were slaves in the triumph, among whom was Gelimer himself, wearing some sort of a purple garment upon his shoulders, and all his family, and as many of the Vandals as were very tall and fair of body. And when Gelimer reached the hippodrome and saw the emperor sitting upon a lofty seat and the people standing on either side and realized as he looked about in what an evil plight he was, he neither wept nor cried out, but ceased not saying over in the words of the Hebrew scripture:[29] "Vanity of vanities, all is vanity." And when he came before the emperor's seat, they stripped off the purple garment, and compelled him to fall prone on the ground and do obeisance to the Emperor Justinian. This also Belisarius did, as being a suppliant of the emperor along with him. And the Emperor Justinian and the Empress Theodora presented the children of Ilderic and his offspring and all those of the family of the Emperor Valentinian with sufficient sums of money, and to Gelimer they gave lands not to be despised in Galatia and permitted him to live there together with his family. However, Gelimer was by no means enrolled among the patricians, since he was unwilling to change from the faith of Arius.

[Jan. 1, 535 A.D.] A little later the triumph[30] was celebrated by, Belisarius in the ancient manner also. For he had the fortune to be advanced to the office of consul, and therefore was borne aloft by the captives, and as he was thus carried in his curule chair, he threw to the populace those very spoils of the Vandalic war. For the people carried off the silver plate and golden girdles and a vast amount of the Vandals' wealth of other sorts as a result of Belisarius' consulship, and it seemed that after a long interval of disuse an old custom was being revived.[31] These things, then, took place in Byzantium in the manner described.


X


And Solomon took over the army in Libya; but in view of the fact that the Moors had risen against him, as has been told previously, and that everything was in suspense, he was at a loss how to treat the situation. For it was reported that the barbarians had destroyed the soldiers in Byzacium and Numidia and that they were pillaging and plundering everything there. But what disturbed most of all both him and all Carthage was the fate which befell Aïgan, the Massagete, and Rufinus, the Thracian, in Byzacium. For both were men of great repute both in the household of Belisarius and in the Roman army, one of them, Aïgan, being among the spearmen of Belisarius, while the other, as the most courageous of all, was accustomed to carry the standard of the general in battle; such an officer the Romans call "bandifer."[32] Now at the time referred to these two men were commanding detachments of cavalry in Byzacium, and when they saw the Moors plundering everything before them and making all the Libyans captives, they watched in a narrow pass with their followers for those who were escorting the booty, and killed them and took away all the captives. And when a report of this came to the commanders of the barbarians, Coutzinas and Esdilasas and Iourphouthes and Medisinissas, who were not far away from this pass, they moved against them with their whole army in the late afternoon. And the Romans, being a very few men and shut off in a narrow place in the midst of many thousands, were not able to ward off their assailants. For wherever they might turn, they were always shot at from the rear. Then, indeed, Rufinus and Aïgan with some few men ran to the top of a rock which was near by and from there defended themselves against the barbarians. Now as long as they were using their bows, the enemy did not dare come directly to a hand-to-hand struggle with them, but they kept hurling their javelins among them; but when all the arrows of the Romans were now exhausted, the Moors closed with them, and they defended themselves with their swords as well as the circumstances permitted. But since they were overpowered by the multitude of the barbarians, Aïgan fell there with his whole body hacked to pieces, and Rufinus was seized by the enemy and led away. But straightway one of the commanders, Medisinissas, fearing lest he should escape and again make trouble for them, cut off his head and taking it to his home shewed it to his wives, for it was a remarkable sight on account of the extraordinary size of the head and the abundance of hair. And now, since the narration of the history has brought me to this point, it is necessary to tell from the beginning whence the nations of the Moors came to Libya and how they settled there.

When the Hebrews had withdrawn from Egypt and had come near the boundaries of Palestine, Moses, a wise man, who was their leader on the journey, died, and the leadership was passed on to Joshua, the son of Nun, who led this people into Palestine, and, by displaying a valour in war greater than that natural to a man, gained possession of the land. And after overthrowing all the nations he easily won the cities, and he seemed to be altogether invincible. Now at that time the whole country along the sea from Sidon as far as the boundaries of Egypt was called Phoenicia. And one king in ancient times held sway over it, as is agreed by all who have written the earliest accounts of the Phoenicians. In that country there dwelt very populous tribes, the Gergesites and the Jebusites and some others with other names by which they are called in the history of the Hebrews.[33] Now when these nations saw that the invading general was an irresistible prodigy, they emigrated from their ancestral homes and made their way to Egypt, which adjoined their country. And finding there no place sufficient for them to dwell in, since there has been a great population in Aegypt from ancient times, they proceeded to Libya. And they established numerous cities and took possession of the whole of Libya as far as the Pillars of Heracles, and there they have lived even up to my time, using the Phoenician tongue. They also built a fortress in Numidia, where now is the city called Tigisis. In that place are two columns made of white stone near by the great spring, having Phoenician letters cut in them which say in the Phoenician tongue: "We are they who fled from before the face of Joshua, the robber, the son of Nun." There were also other nations settled in Libya before the Moors, who on account of having been established there from of old were said to be children of the soil. And because of this they said that Antaeus, their king, who wrestled with Heracles in Clipea,[34] was a son of the earth. And in later times those who removed from Phoenicia with Dido came to the inhabitants of Libya as to kinsmen. And they willingly allowed them to found and hold Carthage. But as time went on Carthage became a powerful and populous city. And a battle took place between them and their neighbours, who, as has been said, had come from Palestine before them and are called Moors at the present time, and the Carthaginians defeated them and compelled them to live a very great distance away from Carthage. Later on the Romans gained the supremacy over all of them in war, and settled the Moors at the extremity of the inhabited land of Libya, and made the Carthaginians and the other Libyans subject and tributary to themselves. And after this the Moors won many victories over the Vandals and gained possession of the land now called Mauretania, extending from Gadira as far as the boundaries of Caesarea,[35] as well as the most of Libya which remained. Such, then, is the story of the settlement of the Moors in Libya.

XI

Now when Solomon heard what had befallen Rufinus and Aïgan, he made ready for war and wrote as follows to the commanders of the Moors: "Other men than you have even before this had the ill fortune to lose their senses and to be destroyed, men who had no means of judging beforehand how their folly would turn out. But as for you, who have the example near at hand in your neighbours, the Vandals, what in the world has happened to you that you have decided to raise your hands against the great emperor and throw away your own security, and that too when you have given the most dread oaths in writing and have handed over your children as pledges to the agreement? Is it that you have determined to make a kind of display of the fact that you have no consideration either for God or for good faith or for kinship itself or for safety or for any other thing at all? And yet, if such is your practice in matters which concern the divine, in what ally do you put your trust in marching against the emperor of the Romans? And if you are taking the field to the destruction of your children, what in the world is it in behalf of which you have decided to endanger yourselves? But if any repentance has by now entered your hearts for what has already taken place, write to us, that we may satisfactorily arrange with you touching what has already been done; but if your madness has not yet abated, expect a Roman war, which will come upon you together with the oaths which you have violated and the wrong which you are doing to your own children."

Such was the letter which Solomon wrote. And the Moors replied as follows: "Belisarius deluded us with great promises and by this means persuaded us to become subjects of the Emperor Justinian;

but the Romans, while giving us no share in any good thing, expected to have us, though pinched with hunger, as their friends and allies. Therefore it is more fitting that you should be called faithless than that the Moors should be. For the men who break treaties are not those who, when manifestly wronged, bring accusation against their neighbours and turn away from them, but those who expect to keep others in faithful alliance with them and then do them violence. And men make God their enemy, not when they march against others in order to recover their own possessions, but when they get themselves into danger of war by encroaching upon the possessions of others. And as for children, that will be your concern, who are not permitted to marry more than one wife; but with us, who have, it may be, fifty wives living with each of us, offspring of children can never fail."

When Solomon had read this letter, he decided to lead his whole army against the Moors. So after arranging matters in Carthage, he proceeded with all his troops to Byzacium. And when he reached the place which is called Mammes,[36] where the four Moorish commanders, whom I have mentioned a little before,[37] were encamped, he made a stockade for himself. Now there are lofty mountains there, and a level space near the foothills of the mountains, where the barbarians had made preparations for the battle and arranged their fighting order as follows. They formed a circle of their camels, just as, in the previous narrative,[38] I have said Cabaon did, making the front about twelve deep. And they placed the women with the children within the circle; (for among the Moors it is customary to take also a few women, with their children, to battle, and these make the stockades and huts for them and tend the horses skilfully, and have charge of the camels and the food; they also sharpen the iron weapons and take upon themselves many of the tasks in connection with the preparation for battle); and the men themselves took their stand on foot in between the legs of the camels, having shields and swords and small spears which they are accustomed to hurl like javelins. And some of them with their horses remained quietly among the mountains. But Solomon disregarded one half of the circle of the Moors, which was towards the mountain, placing no one there. For he feared lest the enemy on the mountain should come down and those in the circle should turn about and thus make the men drawn up there exposed to attack on both sides in the battle. But against the remainder of the circle he drew up his whole army, and since he saw the most of them frightened and without courage, on account of what had befallen Aïgan and Rufinus, and wishing to admonish them to be of good cheer, he spoke as follows: "Men who have campaigned with Belisarius, let no fear of these men enter your minds, and, if Moors gathered to the number of fifty thousand have already defeated five hundred Romans, let not this stand for you as an example. But call to mind your own valour, and consider that while the Vandals defeated the Moors, you have become masters of the Vandals in war without any effort, and that it is not right that those who have conquered the greater should be terrified before those who are inferior. And indeed of all men the Moorish nation seems to be the most poorly equipped for war's struggle. For the most of them have no armour at all, and those who have shields to hold before themselves have only small ones which are not well made and are not able to turn aside what strikes against them. And after they have thrown those two small spears, if they do not accomplish anything, they turn of their own accord to flight. So that it is possible for you, after guarding against the first attack of the barbarians, to win the victory with no trouble at all. But as to your equipment of arms, you see, of course, how great is the difference between it and that of your opponents. And apart from this, both valour of heart and strength of body and experience in war and confidence because you have already conquered all your enemies, all these advantages you have; but the Moors, being deprived of all these things, put their trust only in their own great throng. And it is easier for a few who are most excellently prepared to conquer a multitude of men not good at warfare than it is for the multitude to defeat them. For while the good soldier has his confidence in himself, the cowardly man generally finds that the very number of those arrayed with him produces a want of room that is full of peril. Furthermore, you are warranted in despising these camels, which cannot fight for the enemy, and when struck by our missiles will, in all probability, become the cause of considerable confusion and disorder among them. And the eagerness for battle which the enemy have acquired on account of their former success will be your ally in the fight. For daring, when it is kept commensurate with one's power, will perhaps be of some benefit even to those who make use of it, but when it exceeds one's power it lends into danger. Bearing these things in mind and despising the enemy, observe silence and order; for by taking thought for these things we shall win the victory over the disorder of the barbarians more easily and with less labour." Thus spoke Solomon.

And the commanders of the Moors also, seeing the barbarians terrified at the orderly array of the Romans, and wishing to recall their host to confidence again, exhorted them in this wise: "That the Romans have human bodies, the kind that yield when struck with iron, we have been taught, O fellow-soldiers, by those of them whom we have recently met, the best of them all, some of whom we have overwhelmed with our spears and killed, and the others we have seized and made our prisoners of war. And not only is this so, but it is now possible to see also that we boast great superiority over them in numbers. And, furthermore, the struggle for us involves the very greatest things, either to be masters of all Libya or to be slaves to these braggarts. It is therefore necessary for us to be in the highest degree brave men at the present time. For it is not expedient that those whose all is at stake should be other than exceedingly courageous. And it behoves us to despise the equipment of arms which the enemy have. For if they come on foot against us, they will not be able to move rapidly, but will be worsted by the agility of the Moors, and their cavalry will be terrified both by the sight of the camels, and by the noise they make, which, rising above the general tumult of battle, will, in all likelihood, throw them into disorder. And if anyone by taking into consideration the victory of the Romans over the Vandals thinks them not to be withstood, he is mistaken in his judgment. For the scales of war are, in the nature of the case, turned by the valour of the commander or by fortune; and Belisarius, who was responsible for their gaining the mastery over the Vandals, has now, thanks to Heaven, been removed out of our way. And, besides, we too have many times conquered the Vandals and stripped them of their power, and have thus made the victory over them a more feasible and an easier task for the Romans. And now we have reason to hope to conquer this enemy also if you shew yourselves brave men in the struggle."

After the officers of the Moors had delivered this exhortation, they began the engagement. And at first there arose great disorder in the Roman army. For their horses were offended by the noise made by the camels and by the sight of them, and reared up and threw off their riders and the most of them fled in complete disorder. And in the meantime the Moors were making sallies and hurling all the small spears which they had in their hands, thus causing the Roman army to be filled with tumult, and they were hitting them with their missiles while they were unable either to defend themselves or to remain in position. But after this, Solomon, observing what was happening, leaped down from his horse himself first and caused all the others to do the same. And when they had dismounted, he commanded the others to stand still, and, holding their shields before them and receiving the missiles sent by the enemy, to remain in their position; but he himself, leading forward not less than five hundred men, made an attack upon the other portion of the circle.[39] These men he commanded to draw their swords and kill the camels which stood at that point. Then the Moors who were stationed there beat a hasty retreat, and the men under Solomon killed about two hundred camels, and straightway, when the camels fell, the circle became accessible to the Romans. And they advanced on the run into the middle of the circle where the women of the Moors were sitting; meanwhile the barbarians in consternation withdrew to the mountain which was close by, and as they fled in complete disorder the Romans followed behind and killed them. And it is said that ten thousand of the Moors perished in this encounter, while all the women together with the children were made slaves. And the soldiers secured as booty all the camels which they had not killed. Thus the Romans with all their plunder went to Carthage to celebrate the festival of triumph.

But the barbarians, being moved with anger, once more took the field in a body against the Romans, leaving behind not one of their number, and they began to overrun the country in Byzacium, sparing none of any age of those who fell in their way. And when Solomon had just marched into Carthage it was reported that the barbarians with a great host had come into Byzacium and were plundering everything there. He therefore departed quickly with his whole army and marched against them. And when he reached Bourgaon, where the enemy were encamped, he remained some days in camp over against them, in order that, as soon as the Moors should get on level ground, he might begin the battle. But since they remained on the mountain, he marshalled his army and arrayed it for battle; the Moors, however, had no intention of ever again engaging in battle with the Romans in level country (for already an irresistible fear had come over them), but on the mountain they hoped to overcome them more easily. Now Mt. Bourgaon is for the most part precipitous and on the side toward the east extremely difficult to ascend, but on the west it is easily accessible and rises in an even slope. And there are two lofty peaks which rise up, forming between them a sort of vale, very narrow, but of incredible depth. Now the barbarians left the peak of the mountain unoccupied, thinking that on this side no hostile movement would be made against them; and they left equally unprotected the space about the foot of the mountain where Bourgaon was easy of access. But at the middle of the ascent they made their camp and remained there, in order that, if the enemy should ascend and begin battle with them, they might at the outset, being on higher ground, shoot down upon their heads. They also had on the mountain many horses, prepared either for flight or for the pursuit, if they should win the battle.

Now when Solomon saw that the Moors were unwilling to fight another battle on the level ground, and also that the Roman army was opposed to making a siege in a desert place, he was eager to come to an encounter with the enemy on Bourgaon. But inasmuch as he saw that the soldiers were stricken with terror because of the multitude of their opponents, which was many times greater than it had been in the previous battle, he called together the army and spoke as follows: "The fear which the enemy feel toward you needs no other arraignment, but voluntarily pleads guilty, bringing forward, as it does, the testimony of its own witnesses. For you see, surely, our opponents gathered in so many tens and tens of thousands, but not daring to come down to the plain and engage with us, unable to feel confidence even in their own selves, but taking refuge in the difficulty of this place. It is therefore not even necessary to address any exhortation to you, at the present time at least. For those to whom both the circumstances and the weakness of the enemy give courage, need not, I think, the additional assistance of words. But of this one thing it will be needful to remind you, that if we fight out this engagement also with brave hearts, it will remain for us, having defeated the Vandals and reduced the Moors to the same fortune, to enjoy all the good things of Libya, having no thought whatever of an enemy in our minds. But as to preventing the enemy from shooting down upon our heads, and providing that no harm come to us from the nature of the place, I myself shall make provision."

After making this exhortation Solomon commanded Theodorus, who led the "excubitores[40]" (for thus the Romans call their guards), to take with him a thousand infantrymen toward the end of the afternoon and with some of the standards to go up secretly on the east side of Bourgaon, where the mountain is most difficult of ascent and, one might say, impracticable, commanding him that, when they arrived near the crest of the mountain, they should remain quietly there and pass the rest of the night, and that at sunrise they should appear above the enemy and displaying the standards commence to shoot. And Theodoras did as directed. And when it was well on in the night, they climbed up the precipitous slope and reached a point near the peak without being noticed either by the Moors or even by any of the Romans; for they were being sent out, it was said, as an advance guard, to prevent anyone from coming to the camp from the outside to do mischief. And at early dawn Solomon with the whole army went up against the enemy to the outskirts of Bourgaon. And when morning had come and the enemy were seen near at hand, the soldiers were completely at a loss, seeing the summit of the mountain no longer unoccupied, as formerly, but covered with men who were displaying Roman standards; for already some daylight was beginning to shew. But when those on the peak began their attack, the Romans perceived that the army was their own and the barbarians that they had been placed between their enemy's forces, and being shot at from both sides and having no opportunity to ward off the enemy, they thought no more of resistance but turned, all of them, to a hasty flight. And since they could neither run up to the top of Bourgaon, which was held by the enemy, nor go to the plain anywhere over the lower slopes of the mountain, since their opponents were pressing upon them from that side, they went with a great rush to the vale and the unoccupied peak, some even with their horses, others on foot. But since they were a numerous throng fleeing in great fear and confusion, they kept killing each other, and as they rushed into the vale, which was exceedingly deep, those who were first were being killed constantly, but their plight could not be perceived by those who were coming up behind. And when the vale became full of dead horses and men, and the bodies made a passage from Bourgaon to the other mountain, then the remainder were saved by making the crossing over the bodies. And there perished in this struggle, among the Moors fifty thousand, as was declared by those of them who survived, but among the Romans no one at all, nor indeed did anyone receive even a wound, either at the hand of the enemy or by any accident happening to him, but they all enjoyed this victory unscathed. All of the leaders of the barbarians also made their escape, except Esdilasas, who received pledges and surrendered himself to the Romans. So great, however, was the multitude of women and children whom the Romans seized as booty, that they would sell a Moorish boy for the price of a sheep to any who wished to buy. And then the remainder of the Moors recalled the saying of their women, to the effect that their nation would be destroyed by a beardless man.[41]

So the Roman army, together with its booty and with Esdilasas, marched into Carthage; and those of the barbarians who had not perished decided that it was impossible to settle in Byzacium, lest they, being few, should be treated with violence by the Libyans who were their neighbours, and with their leaders they went into Numidia and made themselves suppliants of Iaudas, who ruled the Moors in Aurasium.[42] And the only Moors who remained in Byzacium were those led by Antalas, who during this time had kept faith with the Romans and together with his subjects had remained unharmed.


XIII

But during the time when these things were happening in Byzacium, Iaudas, who ruled the Moors in Aurasium, bringing more than thirty thousand fighting men, was plundering the country of Numidia and enslaving many of the Libyans. Now it so happened that Althias[43] in Centuriae was keeping guard over the forts there; and he, being eager to take from the enemy some of their captives, went outside the fort with the Huns who were under his command, to the number of about seventy. And reasoning that he was not able to cope with such a great multitude of Moors with only seventy men, he wished to occupy some narrow pass, so that, while the enemy were marching through it, he might be able to snatch up some of the captives. And since there are no such roads there, because flat plains extend in every direction, he devised the following plan.

There is a city not far distant, named Tigisis, then an unwalled place, but having a great spring at a place which was very closely shut in. Althias therefore decided to take possession of this spring, reasoning that the enemy, compelled by thirst, would surely come there; for there is no other water at all close by. Now it seemed to all upon considering the disparity of the armies that his plan was insane. But the Moors came up feeling very much wearied and greatly oppressed by the heat in the summer weather, and naturally almost overcome by an intense thirst, and they made for the spring with a great rush, having no thought of meeting any obstacle. But when they found the water held by the enemy, they all halted, at a loss what to do, the greatest part of their strength having been already expended because of their desire for water. Iaudas therefore had a parley with Althias and agreed to give him the third part of the booty, on condition that the Moors should all drink. But Althias was by no means willing to accept the proposal, but demanded that he fight with him in single combat for the booty. And this challenge being accepted by Iaudas, it was agreed that if it so fell out that Althias was overcome, the Moors should drink. And the whole Moorish army was rejoiced, being in good hope, since Althias was lean and not tall of body, while Iaudas was the finest and most warlike of all the Moors. Now both of them were, as it happened, mounted. And Iaudas hurled his spear first, but as it was coming toward him Althias succeeded with amazing skill in catching it with his right hand, thus filling Iaudas and the enemy with consternation. And with his left hand he drew his bow instantly, for he was ambidextrous, and hit and killed the horse of Iaudas. And as he fell, the Moors brought another horse for their commander, upon which Iaudas leaped and straightway fled; and the Moorish army followed him in complete disorder. And Althias, by thus taking from them the captives and the whole of the booty, won a great name in consequence of this deed throughout all Libya. Such, then, was the course of these events.

And Solomon, after delaying a short time in Carthage, led his army toward Mt. Aurasium and Iaudas, alleging against him that, while the Roman army was occupied in Byzacium, he had plundered many of the places in Numidia. And this was true. Solomon was also urged on against Iaudas by the other commanders of the Moors, Massonas and Ortaïas, because of their personal enmity; Massonas, because his father Mephanias, who was the father-in-law of Iaudas, had been treacherously slain by him, and Ortaïas, because Iaudas, together with Mastinas, who ruled over the barbarians in Mauretania, had purposed to drive him and all the Moors whom he ruled from the land where they had dwelt from of old. So the Roman army, under the leadership of Solomon, and those of the Moors who came into alliance with them, made their camp on the river Abigas, which flows along by Aurasium and waters the land there. But to Iaudas it seemed inexpedient to array himself against the enemy in the plain, but he made his preparations on Aurasium in such a way as seemed to him would offer most difficulty to his assailants. This mountain is about thirteen days' journey distant from Carthage, and the largest of all known to us. For its circuit is a three days' journey for an unencumbered traveller. And for one wishing to go upon it the mountain is difficult of access and extremely wild, but as one ascends and reaches the level ground, plains are seen and many springs which form rivers and a great number of altogether wonderful parks. And the grain which grows here, and every kind of fruit, is double the size of that produced in all the rest of Libya. And there are fortresses also on this mountain, which are neglected, by reason of the fact that they do not seem necessary to the inhabitants. For since the time when the Moors wrested Aurasium from the Vandals,[44] not a single enemy had until now ever come there or so much as caused the barbarians to be afraid that they would come, but even the populous city of Tamougadis, situated against the mountain on the east at the beginning of the plain, was emptied of its population by the Moors and razed to the ground, in order that the enemy should not only not be able to encamp there, but should not even have the city as an excuse for coming near the mountain. And the Moors of that place held also the land to the west of Aurasium, a tract both extensive and fertile. And beyond these dwelt other nations of the Moors, who were ruled by Ortaïas, who had come, as was stated above, as an ally to Solomon and the Romans. And I have heard this man say that beyond the country which he ruled there was no habitation of men, but desert land extending to a great distance, and that beyond that there are men, not black-skinned like the Moors, but very white in body and fair-haired. So much, then, for these things.

And Solomon, after bribing the Moorish allies with great sums of money and earnestly exhorting them, began the ascent of Mt. Aurasium with the whole army arrayed as for battle, thinking that on that day he would do battle with the enemy and just as he was have the matter out with them according as fortune should wish. Accordingly the soldiers did not even take with them any food, except a little, for themselves and their horses. And after proceeding over very rough ground for about fifty stades, they made a bivouac. And covering a similar distance each day they came on the seventh day to a place where there was an ancient fortress and an ever-flowing stream. The place is called "Shield Mountain" by the Romans in their own tongue.[45] Now it was reported to them that the enemy were encamped there, and when they reached this place and encountered no enemy, they made camp and, preparing themselves for battle, remained there; and three days' time was spent by them in that place. And since the enemy kept altogether out of their way, and their provisions had failed, the thought came to Solomon and to the whole army that there had been some plot against them on the part of the Moors who were their allies; for these Moors were not unacquainted with the conditions of travel on Aurasium, and understood, probably, what had been decided upon by the enemy; they were stealthily going out to meet them each day, it was said, and had also frequently been sent to their country by the Romans to reconnoitre, and had decided to make nothing but false reports, in order, no doubt, that the Romans, with no prior knowledge of conditions, might make the ascent of Mt. Aurasium without supplies for a longer time or without preparing themselves otherwise in the way which would be best. And, all things considered, the Romans were suspicious that an ambush had been set for them by men who were their allies and began to be afraid, reasoning that the Moors are said to be by nature untrustworthy at all times and especially whenever they march as allies with the Romans or any others against Moors. So, remembering these things, and at the same time being pinched by hunger, they withdrew from there with all speed without accomplishing anything, and, upon reaching the plain, constructed a stockade.

After this Solomon established a part of the army in Numidia to serve as a guard and with the remainder went to Carthage, since it was already winter. There he arranged and set everything in order, so that at the beginning of spring he might again march against Aurasium with a larger equipment and, if possible, without Moors as allies. At the same time he prepared generals and another army and a fleet of ships for an expedition against the Moors who dwell in the island of Sardinia; for this island is a large one and flourishing besides, being about two thirds as large as Sicily (for the perimeter of the island makes a journey of twenty days for an unencumbered traveller); and lying, as it does, between Rome and Carthage, it was oppressed by the Moors who dwelt there. For the Vandals in ancient times, being enraged against these barbarians, sent some few of them with their wives to Sardinia and confined them there. But as time went on they seized the mountains which are near Caranalis, at first making plundering expeditions secretly upon those who dwelt round about, but when they became no less than three thousand, they even made their raids openly, and with no desire for concealment plundered all the country there, being called Barbaricini[46] by the natives. It was against these barbarians, therefore, that Solomon was preparing the fleet during that winter. Such, then, was the course of events in Libya.


XIV

And in Italy during these same times the following events took place. Belisarius was sent against Theodatus and the Gothic nation by the Emperor Justinian, and sailing to Sicily he secured this island with no trouble. And the manner in which this was done will be told in the following pages, when the history leads me to the narration of the events in Italy. For it has not seemed to me out of order first to record all the events which happened in Libya and after that to turn to the portion of the history touching Italy and the Goths.

During this winter Belisarius remained in Syracuse and Solomon in Carthage. And it came about during this year that a most dread portent took place. For the sun gave forth its light without brightness, like the moon, during this whole year, and it seemed exceedingly like the sun in eclipse, for the beams it shed were not clear nor such as it is accustomed to shed. And from the time when this thing happened men were free neither from war nor pestilence nor any other thing leading to death. And it was the time when Justinian was in the tenth year of his reign. [536-537 A.D.]

[536 A.D.] At the opening of spring, when the Christians were celebrating the feast which they call Easter, there arose a mutiny among the soldiers in Libya. I shall now tell how it arose and to what end it came.

After the Vandals had been defeated in the battle, as I have told previously,[47] the Roman soldiers took their daughters and wives and made them their own by lawful marriage. And each one of these women kept urging her husband to lay claim to the possession of the lands which she had owned previously, saying that it was not right or fitting if, while living with the Vandals, they had enjoyed these lands, but after entering into marriage with the conquerors of the Vandals they were then to be deprived of their possessions. And having these things in mind, the soldiers did not think that they were bound to yield the lands of the Vandals to Solomon, who wished to register them as belonging to the commonwealth and to the emperor's house and said that while it was not unreasonable that the slaves and all other things of value should go as booty to the soldiers, the land itself belonged to the emperor and the empire of the Romans, which had nourished them and caused them to be called soldiers and to be such, not in order to win for themselves such land as they should wrest from the barbarians who were trespassing on the Roman empire, but that this land might come to the commonwealth, from which both they and all others secured their maintenance. This was one cause of the mutiny. And there was a second, concurrent, cause also, which was no less, perhaps even more, effective in throwing all Libya into confusion. It was as follows: In the Roman army there were, as it happened, not less than one thousand soldiers of the Arian faith; and the most of these were barbarians, some of these being of the Erulian[48] nation. Now these men were urged on to the mutiny by the priests of the Vandals with the greatest zeal. For it was not possible for them to worship God in their accustomed way, but they were excluded both from all sacraments and from all sacred rites. For the Emperor Justinian did not allow any Christian who did not espouse the orthodox faith to receive baptism or any other sacrament. But most of all they were agitated by the feast of Easter, during which they found themselves unable to baptize[49] their own children with the sacred water, or do anything else pertaining to this feast. And as if these things were not sufficient for Heaven, in its eagerness to ruin the fortunes of the Romans, it so fell out that still another thing provided an occasion for those who were planning the mutiny. For the Vandals whom Belisarius took to Byzantium were placed by the emperor in five cavalry squadrons, in order that they might be settled permanently in the cities of the East; he also called them the "Vandals of Justinian," and ordered them to betake themselves in ships to the East. Now the majority of these Vandal soldiers reached the East, and, filling up the squadrons to which they had been assigned, they have been fighting against the Persians up to the present time; but the remainder, about four hundred in number, after reaching Lesbos, waiting until the sails were bellied with the wind, forced the sailors to submission and sailed on till they reached the Peloponnesus. And setting sail from there, they came to land in Libya at a desert place, where they abandoned the ships, and, after equipping themselves, went up to Mt. Aurasium and Mauretania. Elated by their accession, the soldiers who were planning the mutiny formed a still closer conspiracy among themselves. And there was much talk about this in the camp and oaths were already being taken. And when the rest were about to celebrate the Easter festival, the Arians, being vexed by their exclusion from the sacred rites, purposed to attack them vigorously.

And it seemed best to their leading men to kill Solomon in the sanctuary on the first day of the feast, which they call the great day. [March 23, 536 A.D.] And they were fortunate enough not to be found out, since no one disclosed this plan. For though there were many who shared in the horrible plot, no word of it was divulged to any hostile person as the orders were passed around, and thus they succeeded completely in escaping detection, for even the spearmen and guards of Solomon for the most part and the majority of his domestics had become associated with this mutiny because of their desire for the lands. And when the appointed day had now come, Solomon was sitting in the sanctuary, utterly ignorant of his own misfortune. And those who had decided to kill the man went in, and, urging one another with nods, they put their hands to their swords, but they did nothing nevertheless, either because they were filled with awe of the rites then being performed in the sanctuary, or because the fame of the general caused them to be ashamed, or perhaps also some divine power prevented them.

And when the rites on that day had been completely performed and all were betaking themselves homeward, the conspirators began to blame one another with having turned soft-hearted at no fitting time, and they postponed the plot for a second attempt on the following day. And on the next day they acted in the same manner and departed from the sanctuary without doing anything, and entering the market place, they reviled each other openly, and every single man of them called the next one soft-hearted and a demoralizer of the band, not hesitating to censure strongly the respect felt for Solomon. For this reason, indeed, they thought that they could no longer without danger remain in Carthage, inasmuch as they had disclosed their plot to the whole city. The most of them, accordingly, went out of the city quickly and began to plunder the lands and to treat as enemies all the Libyans whom they met; but the rest remained in the city, giving no indication of what their own intentions were but pretending ignorance of the plot which had been formed.

But Solomon, upon hearing what was being done by the soldiers in the country, became greatly disturbed, and ceased not exhorting those in the city and urging them to loyalty toward the emperor. And they at first seemed to receive his words with favour, but on the fifth day, when they heard that those who had gone out were secure in their power, they gathered in the hippodrome and insulted Solomon and the other commanders without restraint. And Theodorus, the Cappadocian, being sent there by Solomon, attempted to dissuade them and win them by kind words, but they listened to nothing of what was said. Now this Theodorus had a certain hostility against Solomon and was suspected of plotting against him. For this reason the mutineers straightway elected him general over them by acclamation, and with him they went with all speed to the palace carrying weapons and raising a great tumult. There they killed another Theodorus, who was commander of the guards, a man of the greatest excellence in every respect and an especially capable warrior. And when they had tasted this blood, they began immediately to kill everyone they met, whether Libyan or Roman, if he were known to Solomon or had money in his hands; and then they turned to plundering, going up into the houses which had no soldiers to defend them and seizing all the most valuable things, until the coming of night, and drunkenness following their toil, made them cease.

And Solomon succeeded in escaping unnoticed into the great sanctuary which is in the palace, and Martinus joined him there in the late afternoon. And when all the mutineers were sleeping, they went out from the sanctuary and entered the house of Theodorus, the Cappadocian, who compelled them to dine although they had no desire to do so, and conveyed them to the harbour and put them on the skiff of a certain ship, which happened to have been made ready there by Martinus. And Procopius also, who wrote this history, was with them, and about five men of the house of Solomon. And after accomplishing three hundred stades they reached Misuas, the ship-yard of Carthage, and, since they had reached safety, Solomon straightway commanded Martinus to go into Numidia to Valerian and the others who shared his command, and endeavour to bring it about that each one of them, if it were in any way possible, should appeal to some of the soldiers known to him, either with money or by other means, and bring them back to loyalty toward the emperor. And he sent a letter to Theodorus, charging him to take care of Carthage and to handle the other matters as should seem possible to him, and he himself with Procopius went to Belisarius at Syracuse. And after reporting everything to him which had taken place in Libya, he begged him to come with all speed to Carthage and defend the emperor, who was suffering unholy treatment at the hands of his own soldiers, Solomon, then, was thus engaged.

XV

But the mutineers, after plundering everything in Carthage, gathered in the plain of Boulla, and chose Stotzas,[50] one of the guards of Martinus, and a passionate and energetic man, as tyrant over them, with the purpose of driving the emperor's commanders out of all Libya and thus gaining control over it. And he armed the whole force, amounting to about eight thousand men, and led them on to Carthage, thinking to win over the city instantly with no trouble. He sent also to the Vandals who had run away from Byzantium with the ships and those who had not gone there with Belisarius in the beginning, either because they had escaped notice, or because those who were taking off the Vandals at that time took no account of them. Now they were not fewer than a thousand, and after no great time they joined Stotzas and the army with enthusiasm. And a great throng of slaves also came to him. And when they drew near Carthage, Stotzas sent orders that the people should surrender the city to him as quickly as possible, on condition of their remaining free from harm. But those in Carthage and Theodorus, in reply to this, refused flatly to obey, and announced that they were guarding Carthage for the emperor. And they sent to Stotzas Joseph, the secretary of the emperor's guards, a man of no humble birth and one of the household of Belisarius, who had recently been sent to Carthage on some mission to them, and they demanded that Stotzas should go no further in his violence. But Stotzas, upon hearing this, straightway killed Joseph and commenced a siege. And those in the city, becoming terrified at the danger, were purposing to surrender themselves and Carthage to Stotzas under an agreement. Such was the course of events in the army in Libya.

But Belisarius selected one hundred men from his own spearmen and guards, and taking Solomon with him, sailed into Carthage with one ship at about dusk, at the time when the besiegers were expecting that the city would be surrendered to them on the following day. And since they were expecting this, they bivouacked that night. But when day had come and they learned that Belisarius was present, they broke up camp as quickly as possible and disgracefully and in complete disorder beat a hasty retreat And Belisarius gathered about two thousand of the army and, after urging them with words to be loyal to the emperor and encouraging them with large gifts of money, he began the pursuit of the fugitives. And he overtook them at the city of Membresa, three hundred and fifty stades distant from Carthage. There both armies made camp and prepared themselves for battle, the forces of Belisarius making their entrenchment at the River Bagradas, and the others in a high and difficult position. For neither of them saw fit to enter the city, since it was without walls. And on the day following they joined battle, the mutineers trusting in their numbers, and the troops of Belisarius despising their enemy as both without sense and without generals. And Belisarius, wishing that these thoughts should be firmly lodged in the minds of his soldiers, called them all together and spoke as follows:

"The situation, fellow-soldiers, both for the emperor and for the Romans, falls far short of our hopes and of our prayers. For we have now come to a combat in which even the winning of the victory will not be without tears for us, since we are fighting against kinsmen and men who have been reared with us. But we have this comfort in our misfortune, that we are not ourselves beginning the battle, but have been brought into the conflict in our own defence. For he who has framed the plot against his dearest friends and by his own act has dissolved the ties of kinship, dies not, if he perishes, by the hands of his friends, but having become an enemy is but making atonement to those who have suffered wrong. And that our opponents are public enemies and barbarians and whatever worse name one might call them, is shewn not alone by Libya, which has become plunder under their hands, nor by the inhabitants of this land, who have been wrongfully slain, but also by the multitude of Roman soldiers whom these enemies have dared to kill, though they have had but one fault to charge them with - loyalty to their government. And it is to avenge these their victims that we have now come against them, having with good reason become enemies to those who were once most dear. For nature has made no men in the world either friends or opponents to one another, but it is the actions of men in every case which, either by the similarity of the motives which actuate them unite them in alliance, or by the difference set them in hostility to each other, making them friends or enemies as the case may be. That, therefore, we are fighting against men who are outlaws and enemies of the state, you must now be convinced; and now I shall make it plain that they deserve to be despised by us. For a throng of men united by no law, but brought together by motives of injustice, is utterly unable by nature to play the part of brave men, since valour is unable to dwell with lawlessness, but always shuns those who are unholy. Nor, indeed, will they preserve discipline or give heed to the commands given by Stotzas. For when a tyranny is newly organized and has not yet won that authority which self-confidence gives, it is, of necessity, looked upon by its subjects with contempt. Nor is it honoured through any sentiment of loyalty, for a tyranny is, in the nature of the case, hated; nor does it lead its subjects by fear, for timidity deprives it of the power to speak out openly. And when the enemy is handicapped in point of valour and of discipline, their defeat is ready at hand. With great contempt, therefore, as I said, we should go against this enemy of ours. For it is not by the numbers of the combatants, but by their orderly array and their bravery, that prowess in war is wont to be measured."

So spoke Belisarius. And Stotzas exhorted his troops as follows: "Men who with me have escaped our servitude to the Romans, let no one of you count it unworthy to die on behalf of the freedom which you have won by your courage and your other qualities. For it is not so terrible a thing to grow old and die in the midst of ills, as to return again to it after having gained freedom from oppressive conditions. For the interval which has given one a taste of deliverance makes the misfortune, naturally enough, harder to bear. And this being so, it is necessary for you to call to mind that after conquering the Vandals and the Moors you yourselves have enjoyed the labours of war, while others have become masters of all the spoils. And consider that, as soldiers, you will be compelled all your lives to be acquainted with the dangers of war, either in behalf of the emperor's cause, if, indeed, you are again his slaves, or in behalf of your own selves, if you preserve this present liberty. And whichever of the two is preferable, this it is in your power to choose, either by becoming faint-hearted at this time, or by preferring to play the part of brave men. Furthermore, this thought also should come to your minds, that if, having taken up arms against the Romans, you come under their power, you will have experience of no moderate or indulgent masters, but you will suffer the extreme of punishment, and, what is more, your death will not have been unmerited. To whomsoever of you, therefore, death comes in this battle, it is plain that it will be a glorious death; and life, if you conquer the enemy, will be independent and in all other respects happy; but if you are defeated, I need mention no other bitterness than this, that all your hope will depend upon the mercy of those men yonder. And the conflict will not be evenly matched in regard to strength. For not only are the enemy greatly surpassed by us in numbers, but they will come against us without the least enthusiasm, for I think that they are praying for a share of this our freedom." Such was the speech of Stotzas.

As the armies entered the combat, a wind both violent and exceedingly troublesome began to blow in the faces of the mutineers of Stotzas. For this reason they thought it disadvantageous for them to fight the battle where they were, fearing lest the wind by its overpowering force should carry the missiles of the enemy against them, while the impetus of their own missiles would be very seriously checked. They therefore left their position and moved toward the flank, reasoning that if the enemy also should change front, as they probably would, in order that they might not be assailed from the rear, the wind would then be in their faces. But Belisarius, upon seeing that they had left their position and in complete disorder were moving to his flank, gave orders immediately to open the attack. And the troops of Stotzas were thrown into confusion by the unexpected move, and in great disorder, as each one could, they fled precipitately, and only when they reached Numidia did they collect themselves again. Few of them, however, perished in this action, and most of them were Vandals. For Belisarius did not pursue them at all, for the reason that it seemed to him sufficient, since his army was very small, if the enemy, having been defeated for the present, should get out of his way. And he gave the soldiers the enemy's stockade to plunder, and they took it with not a man inside. But much money was found there and many women, the very women because of whom this war took place.[51] After accomplishing this, Belisarius marched back to Carthage. And someone coming from Sicily reported to him that a mutiny had broken out in the army and was about to throw everything into confusion, unless he himself should return to them with all speed and take measures to prevent it. He there therefore arranged matters in Libya as well as he could and, entrusting Carthage to Ildiger and Theodorus, went to Sicily.

And the Roman commanders in Numidia, hearing that the troops of Stotzas had come and were gathering there, prepared for battle. Now the commanders were as follows: of foederati,[52] Marcellus and Cyril, of the cavalry forces, Barbatus, and of infantry Terentius and Sarapis. All, however, took their commands from Marcellus, as holding the authority in Numidia. He, therefore, upon hearing that Stotzas with some few men was in a place called Gazophyla,[53] about two days' journey distant from Constantina,[54] wished to anticipate the gathering of all the mutineers, and led his army swiftly against them. And when the two armies were near together and the battle was about to commence, Stotzas came alone into the midst of his opponents and spoke as follows:

"Fellow-soldiers, you are not acting justly in taking the field against kinsmen and those who have been reared with you, and in raising arms against men who in vexation at your misfortunes and the wrongs you have suffered have decided to make war upon the emperor and the Romans. Or do you not remember that you have been deprived of the pay which has been owing you for a long time back, and that you have been robbed of the enemy's spoil, which the law of war has set as prizes for the dangers of battle? And that the others have claimed the right to live sumptuously all their lives upon the good things of victory, while you have followed as if their servants? If, now, you are angry with me, it is within your power to vent your wrath upon this body, and to escape the pollution of killing the others; but if you have no charge to bring against me, it is time for you to take up your weapons in your own behalf." So spoke Stotzas; and the soldiers listened to his words and greeted him with great favour. And when the commanders saw what was happening, they withdrew in silence and took refuge in a sanctuary which was in Gazophyla. And Stotzas combined both armies into one and then went to the commanders. And finding them in the sanctuary, he gave pledges and then killed them all.

XVI

When the emperor learned this, he sent his nephew Germanus, a man of patrician rank, with some few men to Libya. And Symmachus also and Domnicus, men of the senate, followed him, the former to be prefect and charged with the maintenance of the army, while Domnicus was to command the infantry forces. For John,[55] who had held the office of prefect, had already died of disease. And when they had sailed into Carthage, Germanus counted the soldiers whom they had, and upon looking over the books of the scribes where the names of all the soldiers were registered, he found that the third part of the army was in Carthage and the other cities, while all the rest were arrayed with the tyrant against the Romans. He did not, therefore, begin any fighting, but bestowed the greatest care upon his army. And considering that those left in Carthage were the kinsmen or tentmates of the enemy, he kept addressing many winning words to all, and in particular said that he had himself been sent by the emperor to Libya in order to defend the soldiers who had been wronged and to punish those who had unprovoked done them any injury. And when this was found out by the mutineers, they began to come over to him a few at a time. And Germanus both received them into the city in a friendly manner and, giving pledges, held them in honour, and he gave them their pay for the time during which they had been in arms against the Romans. And when the report of these acts was circulated and came to all, they began now to detach themselves in large numbers from the tyrant and to march to Carthage. Then at last Germanus, hoping that in the battle he would be evenly matched in strength with his opponents, began to make preparations for the conflict.

But in the meantime Stotzas, already perceiving the trouble, and fearing lest by the defection of still others of his soldiers the army should be reduced still more, was pressing for a decisive encounter immediately and trying to take hold of the war with more vigour. And since he had some hope regarding the soldiers in Carthage, that they would come over to him, and thought that they would readily desert if he came near them, he held out the hope to all his men; and after encouraging them exceedingly in this way, he advanced swiftly with his whole army against Carthage. And when he had come within thirty-five stades of the city, he made camp not far from the sea, and Germanus, after arming his whole army and arraying them for battle, marched forth. And when they were all outside the city, since he had heard what Stotzas was hoping for, he called together the whole army and spoke as follows:

"That there is nothing, fellow-soldiers, with which you can justly reproach the emperor, and no fault which you can find with what he has done to you, this, I think, no one of you all could deny; for it was he who took you as you came from the fields with your wallets and one small frock apiece and brought you together in Byzantium, and has caused you to be so powerful that the Roman state now depends upon you. And that he has not only been treated with wanton insult, but has also suffered the most dreadful of all things at your hands, you yourselves, doubtless, know full well. And desiring that you should preserve the memory of these things for ever, he has dismissed the accusations brought against you for your crimes, asking that this debt alone be due to him from you, shame for what you have done. It is reasonable, therefore, that you, being thus regarded by him, should learn anew the lesson of good faith and correct your former folly. For when repentance comes at the fitting time upon those who have done wrong, it is accustomed to make those who have been injured indulgent; and service which comes in season is wont to bring another name to those who have been called ungrateful.

"And it will be needful for you to know well this also, that if at the present time you shew yourselves completely loyal to the emperor, no remembrance will remain of what has gone before. For in the nature of things every course of action is characterized by men in accordance with its final outcome; and while a wrong which has once been committed can never be undone in all time, still, when it has been corrected by better deeds on the part of those who committed it, it receives the fitting reward of silence and generally comes to be forgotten. Moreover, if you act with any disregard of duty toward these accursed rascals at the present time, even though afterwards you fight through many wars in behalf of the Romans and often win the victory over the enemy, you will never again be regarded as having requited the emperor as you can requite him to-day. For those who win applause in the very matter of their former wrong-doing always gain for themselves a fairer apology. As regards the emperor, then, let each one of you reason in some such way. But as for me, I have not voluntarily done you any injustice, and I have displayed my good-will to you by all possible means, and now, facing this danger, I have decided to ask this much of you all: let no man advance with us against the enemy contrary to his judgement. But if anyone of you is already desirous of arraying himself with them, without delay let him go with his weapons to the enemy's camp, granting us this one favour, that it be not stealthily, but openly, that he has decided to do us wrong. Indeed, it is for this reason that I am making my speech, not in Carthage, but after coming on the battle-field, in order that I might not be an obstacle to anyone who desires to desert to our opponents, since it is possible for all without danger to shew their disposition toward the state." Thus spoke Germanus. And a great uproar ensued in the Roman army, for each one demanded the right to be the first to display to the general his loyalty to the emperor and to swear the most dread oaths in confirmation.


## XVII

Now for some time the two armies remained in position opposite each other. But when the mutineers saw that nothing of what Stotzas had foretold was coming to pass, they began to be afraid as having been unexpectedly cheated of their hope, and they broke their ranks and withdrew, and marched off to Numidia, where were their women and the money from their booty. And Germanus too came there with the whole army not long afterwards, having made all preparations in the best way possible and also bringing along many wagons for the army. And overtaking his opponents in a place which the Romans call Scalae Veteres, he made his preparations for battle in the following manner. Placing the wagons in line facing the front, he arrayed all the infantry along them under the leadership of Domnicus, so that by reason of having their rear in security they might fight with the greater courage. And the best of the horsemen and those who had come with him from Byzantium he himself had on the left of the infantry, while all the others he placed on the right wing, not marshalled in one body but in three divisions. And Ildiger led one of them, Theodoras the Cappadocian another, while the remaining one, which was larger, was commanded by John, the brother of Pappus, with three others. Thus did the Romans array themselves.

And the mutineers took their stand opposite them, not in order, however, but scattered, more in the manner of barbarians. And at no great distance many thousands of Moors followed them, who were commanded by a number of leaders, and especially by Iaudas and Ortaïas. But not all of them, as it happened, were faithful to Stotzas and his men, for many had sent previously to Germanus and agreed that, when they came into the fight, they would array themselves with the emperor's army against the enemy. However, Germanus could not trust them altogether, for the Moorish nation is by nature faithless to all men. It was for this reason also that they did not array themselves with the mutineers, but remained behind, waiting for what would come to pass, in order that with those who should be victorious they might join in the pursuit of the vanquished. Such was the purpose, then, of the Moors, in following behind and not mingling with the mutineers.

And when Stotzas came close to the enemy and saw the standard of Germanus, he exhorted his men and began to charge against him. But the mutinous Eruli who were arrayed about him did not follow and even tried with all their might to prevent him, saying that they did not know the character of the forces of Germanus, but that they did know that those arrayed on the enemy's right would by no means withstand them. If, therefore, they should advance against these, they would not only give way themselves and turn to flight, but would also, in all probability, throw the rest of the Roman army into confusion; but if they should attack Germanus and be driven back and put to rout, their whole cause would be ruined on the spot. And Stotzas was persuaded by these words, and permitted the others to fight with the men of Germanus, while he himself with the best men went against John and those arrayed with him. And they failed to withstand the attack and hastened to flee in complete disorder. And the mutineers took all their standards immediately, and pursued them as they fled at top speed, while some too charged upon the infantry, who had already begun to abandon their ranks. But at this juncture Germanus himself, drawing his sword and urging the whole of that part of the army to do the same, with great difficulty routed the mutineers opposed to him and advanced on the run against Stotzas. And then, since he was joined in this effort by the men of Ildiger and Theodorus, the two armies mingled with each other in such a way that, while the mutineers were pursuing some of their enemy, they were being overtaken and killed by others. And as the confusion became greater and greater, the troops of Germanus, who were in the rear, pressed on still more, and the mutineers, falling into great fear, thought no longer of resistance. But neither side could be distinguished either by their own comrades or by their opponents. For all used one language and the same equipment of arms, and they differed neither in figure nor in dress nor in any other thing whatever. For this reason the soldiers of the emperor by the advice of Germanus, whenever they captured anyone, asked who he was; and then, if he said that he was a soldier of Germanus, they bade him give the watchword of Germanus, and if he was not at all able to give this, they killed him instantly. In this struggle one of the enemy got by unnoticed and killed the horse of Germanus, and Germanus himself fell to the ground and came into danger, and would have been lost had not his guards quickly saved him by forming an enclosure around him and mounting him on another horse.

As for Stotzas, he succeeded in this tumult in escaping with a few men. But Germanus, urging on his men, went straight for the enemy's camp. There he was encountered by those of the mutineers who had been stationed to guard the stockade. A stubborn fight took place around its entrance, and the mutineers came within a little of forcing back their opponents, but Germanus sent some of his followers and bade them make trial of the camp at another point. These men, since no one was defending the camp at this place, got inside the stockade with little trouble. And the mutineers, upon seeing them, rushed off in flight, and Germanus with all the rest of the army dashed into the enemy's camp. There the soldiers, finding it easy to plunder the goods of the camp, neither took any account of the enemy nor paid any further heed to the exhortations of their general, since booty was at hand. For this reason Germanus, fearing lest the enemy should get together and come upon them, himself with some few men took his stand at the entrance of the stockade, uttering many laments and urging his unheeding men to return to good order. And many of the Moors, when the rout had taken place in this way, were now pursuing the mutineers, and, arraying themselves with the emperor's troops, were plundering the camp of the vanquished. But Stotzas, at first having confidence in the Moorish army, rode to them in order to renew the battle. But perceiving what was being done, he fled with a hundred men, and succeeded with difficulty in making his escape. And once more many gathered about him and attempted to engage with the enemy, but being repulsed no less decisively than before, if not even more so, they all came over to Germanus. And Stotzas alone with some few Vandals withdrew to Mauretania, and taking to wife the daughter of one of the rulers, remained there. And this was the conclusion of that mutiny.

XVIII

Now there was among the body-guards of Theodorus, the Cappadocian, a certain Maximinus, an exceedingly base man. This Maximinus had first got a very large number of the soldiers to join with him in a conspiracy against the government, and was now purposing to attempt a tyranny. And being eager to associate with himself still more men, he explained the project to others and especially to Asclepiades, a native of Palestine, who was a man of good birth and the first of the personal friends of Theodorus. Now Asclepiades, after conversing with Theodorus, straightway reported the whole matter to Germanus. And he, not wishing as yet, while affairs were still unsettled, to begin any other disturbance, decided to get the best of the man by cajoling and flattering him rather than by punishment, and to bind him by oaths to loyalty toward the government. Accordingly, since it was an old custom among all Romans that no one should become a body-guard of one of the commanders, unless he had previously taken the most dread oaths and given pledges of his loyalty both toward his own commander and toward the Roman emperor, he summoned Maximinus, and praising him for his daring, directed him to be one of his body-guards from that time forth. And he, being overjoyed at the extraordinary honour, and conjecturing that his project would in this way get on more easily, took the oath, and though from that time forth he was counted among the body-guards of Germanus, he did not hesitate to disregard his oaths immediately and to strengthen much more than ever his plans to achieve the tyranny.

Now the whole city was celebrating some general festival, and many of the conspirators of Maximinus at about the time of lunch came according to their agreement to the palace, where Germanus was entertaining his friends at a feast, and Maximinus took his stand beside the couches with the other body-guards. And as the drinking proceeded, someone entered and announced to Germanus that many soldiers were standing in great disorder before the door of the court, putting forward the charge that the government owed them their pay for a long period. And he commanded the most trusty of the guards secretly to keep close watch over Maximinus, allowing him in no way to perceive what was being done. Then the conspirators with threats and tumult proceeded on the run to the hippodrome, and those who shared their plan with them gathered gradually from the houses and were assembling there. And if it had so chanced that all of them had come together, no one, I think, would have been able easily to destroy their power; but, as it was, Germanus anticipated this, and, before the greater part had yet arrived, he straightway sent against them all who were well-disposed to himself and to the emperor. And they attacked the conspirators before they expected them. And then, since Maximinus, for whom they were waiting to begin the battle for them, was not with them, and they did not see the crowd gathered to help them, as they had thought it would be, but instead even beheld their fellow-soldiers unexpectedly fighting against them, they consequently lost heart and were easily overcome in the struggle and rushed off in flight and in complete disorder. And their opponents slew many of them, and they also captured many alive and brought them to Germanus. Those, however, who had not already come to the hippodrome gave no indication of their sentiment toward Maximinus. And Germanus did not see fit to go on and seek them out, but he enquired whether Maximinus, since he had sworn the oath, had taken part in the plot. And since it was proved that, though numbered among his own body-guards he had carried on his designs still more than before, Germanus impaled him close by the fortifications of Carthage, and in this way succeeded completely in putting down the sedition. As for Maximinus, then, such was the end of his plot.


XIX

[539-540 A.D.] And the emperor summoned Germanus together with Symmachus and Domnicus and again entrusted all Libya to Solomon, in the thirteenth year of his reign; and he provided him with an army and officers, among whom were Rufinus and Leontius, the sons of Zaunas the son of Pharesmanas, and John, the son of Sisiniolus. For Martinus and Valerianus had already before this gone under summons to Byzantium. And Solomon sailed to Carthage, and having rid himself of the sedition of Stotzas, he ruled with moderation and guarded Libya securely, setting the army in order, and sending to Byzantium and to Belisarius whatever suspicious elements he found in it, and enrolling new soldiers to equal their number, and removing those of the Vandals who were left and especially all their women from the whole of Libya. And he surrounded each city with a wall, and guarding the laws with great strictness, he restored the government completely. And Libya became under his rule powerful as to its revenues and prosperous in other respects.

And when everything had been arranged by him in the best way possible, he again made an expedition against Iaudas and the Moors on Aurasium. And first he sent forward Gontharis, one of his own body-guards and an able warrior, with an army. Now Gontharis came to the Abigas River and made camp near Bagaïs, a deserted city. And there he engaged with the enemy, but was defeated in battle, and retiring to his stockade was already being hard pressed by the siege of the Moors. But afterwards Solomon himself arrived with his whole army, and when he was sixty stades away from the camp which Gontharis was commanding, he made a stockade and remained there; and hearing all that had befallen the force of Gontharis, he sent them a part of his army and bade them keep up the fight against the enemy with courage. But the Moors, having gained the upper hand in the engagement, as I have said, did as follows. The Abigas River flows from Aurasium, and descending into a plain, waters the land just as the men there desire. For the natives conduct this stream to whatever place they think it will best serve them at the moment, for in this plain there are many channels, into which the Abigas is divided, and entering all of them, it passes underground, and reappears again above the ground and gathers its stream together. This takes place over the greatest part of the plain and makes it possible for the inhabitants of the region, by stopping up the waterways with earth, or by again opening them, to make use of the waters of this river as they wish. So at that time the Moors shut off all the channels there and thus allowed the whole stream to flow about the camp of the Romans. As a result of this, a deep, muddy marsh formed there through which it was impossible to go; this terrified them exceedingly and reduced them to a state of helplessness. When this was heard by Solomon, he came quickly. But the barbarians, becoming afraid, withdrew to the foot of Aurasium. And in a place which they call Babosis they made camp and remained there. So Solomon moved with his whole army and came to that place. And upon engaging with the enemy, he defeated them decisively and turned them to flight. Now after this the Moors did not think it advisable for them to fight a pitched battle with the Romans; for they did not hope to overcome them in this kind of contest; but they did have hope, based on the difficult character of the country around Aurasium, that the Romans would in a short time give up by reason of the sufferings they would have to endure and would withdraw from there, just as they formerly had done. The most of them, therefore, went off to Mauretania and the barbarians to the south of Aurasium, but Iaudas with twenty thousand of the Moors remained there. And it happened that he had built a fortress on Aurasium, Zerboule by name. Into this he entered with all the Moors and remained quiet. But Solomon was by no means willing that time should be wasted in the siege, and learning that the plains about the city of Tamougade were full of grain just becoming ripe, he led his army into them, and settling himself there, began to plunder the land. Then, after firing everything, he returned again to the fortress of Zerboule.

But during this time, while the Romans were plundering the land, Iaudas, leaving behind some of the Moors, about as many as he thought would be sufficient for the defence of the fortress, himself ascended to the summit of Aurasium with the rest of the army, not wishing to stand siege in the fort and have provisions fail his forces. And finding a high place with cliff's on all sides of it and concealed by perpendicular rocks, Toumar by name, he remained quietly there. And the Romans besieged the fortress of Zerboule for three days. And using their bows, since the wall was not high, they hit many of the barbarians upon the parapets. And by some chance it happened that all the leaders of the Moors were hit by these missiles and died. And when the three days' time had passed and night came on, the Romans, having learned nothing of the death of the leaders among the Moors, were planning to break up the siege. For it seemed better to Solomon to go against Iaudas and the multitude of the Moors, thinking that, if he should be able to capture that force by siege, the barbarians in Zerboule would with less trouble and difficulty yield to the Romans. But the barbarians, thinking that they could no longer hold out against the siege, since all their leaders had now been destroyed, decided to flee with all speed and abandon the fortress. Accordingly they fled immediately in silence and without allowing the enemy in any way to perceive it, and the Romans also at daybreak began to prepare for departure. And since no one appeared on the wall, although the besieging army was withdrawing, they began to wonder and fell into the greatest perplexity among themselves. And in this state of uncertainty they went around the fortress and found the gate open from which the Moors had departed in flight. And entering the fortress they treated everything as plunder, but they had no thought of pursuing the enemy, for they had set out with light equipment and were familiar with the country round about. And when they had plundered everything, they set guards over the fortress, and all moved forward on foot.

And coming to the place Toumar, where the enemy had shut themselves in and were remaining quiet, they encamped near by in a bad position, where there would be no supply of water, except a little, nor any other necessary thing. And after much time had been spent and the barbarians did not come out against them at all, they themselves, no less than the enemy, if not even more, were hard pressed by the siege and began to be impatient. And more than anything else, they were distressed by the lack of water; this Solomon himself guarded, giving each day no more than a single cupful to each man. And since he saw that they were openly discontented and no longer able to bear their present hardships, he planned to make trial of the place, although it was difficult of access, and called all together and exhorted them as follows: "Since God has granted to the Romans to besiege the Moors on Aurasium, a thing which hitherto has been beyond hope and now, to such as do not see what is actually being done, is altogether incredible, it is necessary that we too should lend our aid to the help that has come from above, and not prove false to this favour, but undergoing the danger with enthusiasm, should reach after the good fortune which is to come from success. For in every case the turning of the scales of human affairs depends upon the moment of opportunity; but if a man, by wilful cowardice, is traitor to his fortune, he cannot justly blame it, having by his own action brought the guilt upon himself. Now as for the Moors, you see their weakness surely and the place in which they have shut themselves up and are keeping guard, deprived of all the necessities of life. And as for you, one of two things is necessary, either without feeling any vexation at the siege to await the surrender of the enemy, or, if you shrink from this, to accept the victory which goes with the danger. And fighting against these barbarians will be the more free from danger for us, inasmuch as they are already fighting with hunger and I think they will never even come to an engagement with us. Having these things in mind at the present time, it behooves you to execute all your orders with eagerness."

After Solomon had made this exhortation, he looked about to see from what point it would be best for his men to make an attempt on the place, and for a long time he seemed to be in perplexity. For the difficult nature of the ground seemed to him quite too much to contend with. But while Solomon was considering this, chance provided a way for the enterprise as follows. There was a certain Gezon in the army, a foot-soldier, "optio"[56] of the detachment to which Solomon belonged; for thus the Romans call the paymaster. This Gezon, either in play or in anger, or perhaps even moved by some divine impulse, began to make the ascent alone, apparently going against the enemy, and not far from him went some of his fellow-soldiers, marvelling greatly at what he was doing. And three of the Moors, who had been stationed to guard the approach, suspecting that the man was coming against them, went on the run to confront him. But since they were in a narrow way, they did not proceed in orderly array, but each one went separately. And Gezon struck the first one who came upon him and killed him, and in this way he despatched each of the others. And when those in the rear perceived this, they advanced with much shouting and tumult against the enemy. And when the whole Roman army both heard and saw what was being done, without waiting either for the general to lead the way for them or for the trumpets to give the signal for battle, as was customary, nor indeed even keeping their order, but making a great uproar and urging one another on, they ran against the enemy's camp. There Rufinus and Leontius, the sons of Zaunas the son of Pharesmanes, made a splendid display of valorous deeds against the enemy. And by this the Moors were terror-stricken, and when they learned that their guards also had been destroyed, they straightway turned to flight where each one could, and the most of them were overtaken in the difficult ground and killed. And Iaudas himself, though struck by a javelin in the thigh, still made his escape and withdrew to Mauretania. But the Romans, after plundering the enemy's camp, decided not to abandon Aurasium again, but to guard fortresses which Solomon was to build there, so that this mountain might not be again accessible to the Moors.

Now there is on Aurasium a perpendicular rock which rises in the midst of precipices; the natives call it the Rock of Geminianus; there the men of ancient times had built a tower, making it very small as a place of refuge, strong and unassailable, since the nature of the position assisted them. Here, as it happened, Iaudas had a few days previously deposited his money and his women, setting one old Moor in charge as guardian of the money. For he could never have suspected that the enemy would either reach this place, or that they could in all time capture the tower by force. But the Romans at that time, searching through the rough country of Aurasium, came there, and one of them, with a laugh, attempted to climb up to the tower; but the women began to taunt him, ridiculing him as attempting the impossible; and the old man, peering out from the tower, did the same thing. But when the Roman soldier, climbing with both hands and feet, had come near them, he drew his sword quietly and leaped forward as quickly as he could, and struck the old man a fair blow on the neck, and succeeded in cutting it through. And the head fell down to the ground, and the soldiers, now emboldened and holding to one another, ascended to the tower, and took out from there both the women and the money, of which there was an exceedingly great quantity. And by means of it Solomon surrounded many of the cities in Libya with walls.

And after the Moors had retired from Numidia, defeated in the manner described, the land of Zabe, which is beyond Mt. Aurasium and is called "First Mauretania," whose metropolis is Sitiphis,[57] was added to the Roman empire by Solomon as a tributary province; for of the other Mauretania Caesarea is the first city, where was settled Mastigas[58] with his Moors, having the whole country there subject and tributary to him, except, indeed, the city of Caesarea. For this city Belisarius had previously recovered for the Romans, as has been set forth in the previous narrative[59]; and the Romans always journey to this city in ships, but they are not able to go by land, since Moors dwell in that country. And as a result of this all the Libyans who were subjects of the Romans, coming to enjoy secure peace and finding the rule of Solomon wise and very moderate, and having no longer any thought of hostility in their minds, seemed the most fortunate of all men.


XXI

But in the fourth year after this it came about that all their blessings were turned to the opposite. [543-544 A.D.] For in the seventeenth year of the reign of the Emperor Justinian, Cyrus and Sergius, the sons of Bacchus, Solomon's brother, were assigned by the emperor to rule over the cities in Libya, Cyrus, the elder, to have Pentapolis,[60] and Sergius Tripolis. And the Moors who are called Leuathae came to Sergius with a great army at the city of Leptimagna,[61] spreading the report that the reason they had come was this, that Sergius might give them the gifts and insignia of office which were customary[62] and so make the peace secure. But Sergius, persuaded by Pudentius, a man of Tripolis, of whom I made mention in the preceding narrative[63] as having served the Emperor Justinian against the Vandals at the beginning of the Vandalic War, received eighty of the barbarians, their most notable men, into the city, promising to fulfil all their demands; but he commanded the rest to remain in the suburb. Then after giving these eighty men pledges concerning the peace, he invited them to a banquet. But they say that these barbarians had come into the city with treacherous intent, that they might lay a trap for Sergius and kill him. And when they came into conference with him, they called up many charges against the Romans, and in particular said that their crops had been plundered wrongfully. And Sergius, paying no heed to these things, rose from the seat on which he was sitting, with intent to go away. And one of the barbarians, laying hold upon his shoulder, attempted to prevent him from going. Then the others began to shout in confusion, and were already rushing together about him. But one of the body-guards of Sergius, drawing his sword, despatched that Moor. And as a result of this a great tumult, as was natural, arose in the room, and the guards of Sergius killed all the barbarians. But one of them, upon seeing the others being slain, rushed out of the house where these things were taking place, unnoticed by anyone, and coming to his tribemates, revealed what had befallen their fellows. And when they heard this, they betook themselves on the run to their own camp and together with all the others arrayed themselves in arms against the Romans. Now when they came near the city of Leptimagna, Sergius and Pudentius confronted them with their whole army. And the battle becoming a hand-to-hand fight, at first the Romans were victorious and slew many of the enemy, and, plundering their camp, secured their goods and enslaved an exceedingly great number of women and children. But afterwards Pudentius, being possessed by a spirit of reckless daring, was killed; and Sergius with the Roman army, since it was already growing dark, marched into Leptimagna.

At a later time the barbarians took the field against the Romans with a greater array. And Sergius went to join his uncle Solomon, in order that he too might go to meet the enemy with a larger army; and he found there his brother Cyrus also. And the barbarians, coming into Byzacium, made raids and plundered a great part of the country there; and Antalas (whom I mentioned in the preceding narrative[64] as having remained faithful to the Romans and as being for this reason sole ruler of the Moors in Byzacium) had by now, as it happened, become hostile to Solomon, because Solomon had deprived him of the maintenance with which the emperor had honoured him and had killed his brother, charging him with responsibility for an uprising against the people of Byzacium. So at that time Antalas was pleased to see these barbarians, and making an offensive and defensive alliance with them, led them against Solomon and Carthage.

And Solomon, as soon as he heard about this, put his whole army in motion and marched against them, and coming upon them at the city of Tebesta, distant six days' journey from Carthage, he established his camp in company with the sons of his brother Bacchus, Cyrus and Sergius and Solomon the younger. And fearing the multitude of the barbarians, he sent to the leaders of the Leuathae, reproaching them because, while at peace with the Romans, they had taken up arms and come against them, and demanding that they should confirm the peace existing between the two peoples, and he promised to swear the most dread oaths, that he would hold no remembrance of what they had done. But the barbarians, mocking his words, said that he would of course swear by the sacred writings of the Christians, which they are accustomed to call Gospels. Now since Sergius had once taken these oaths and then had slain those who trusted in them,[65] it was their desire to go into battle and make a test of these same sacred writings, to see what sort of power they had against the perjurers, in order that they might first have absolute confidence in them before they finally entered into the agreement. When Solomon heard this, he made his preparations for the combat.

And on the following day he engaged with a portion of the enemy as they were bringing in a very large booty, conquered them in battle, seized all their booty and kept it under guard. And when the soldiers were dissatisfied and counted it an outrage that he did not give them the plunder, he said that he was awaiting the outcome of the war, in order that they might distribute everything then, according to the share that should seem to suit the merit of each. But when the barbarians advanced a second time, with their whole army, to give battle, this time some of the Romans stayed behind and the others entered the encounter with no enthusiasm. At first, then, the battle was evenly contested, but later, since the Moors were vastly superior by reason of their great numbers, the most of the Romans fled, and though Solomon and a few men about him held out for a time against the missiles of the barbarians, afterwards they were overpowered by the enemy, and fleeing in haste, reached a ravine made by a brook which flowed in that region. And there Solomon's horse stumbled and threw him to the ground, and his body-guards lifted him quickly in their arms and set him upon his horse. But overcome by great pain and unable to hold the reins longer, he was overtaken and killed by the barbarians, and many of his guards besides. Such was the end of Solomon's life.


## XXII

After the death of Solomon, Sergius, who, as has been said, was his nephew, took over the government of Libya by gift of the emperor. And this man became the chief cause of great ruin to the people of Libya, and all were dissatisfied with his rule, the officers because, being exceedingly stupid and young both in character and in years, he proved to be the greatest braggart of all men, and he insulted them for no just cause and disregarded them, always using the power of his wealth and the authority of his office to this end; and the soldiers disliked him because he was altogether unmanly and weak; and the Libyans, not only for these reasons, but also because he had shown himself strangely fond of the wives and the possessions of others. But most of all John, the son of Sisiniolus, was hostile to the power of Sergius; for, though he was an able warrior and was a man of unusually fair repute, he found Sergius absolutely ungrateful. For this reason neither he nor anyone else at all was willing to take up arms against the enemy. But almost all the Moors were following Antalas, and Stotzas came at his summons from Mauretania. And since not one of the enemy came out against them, they began to sack the country, making plunder of everything without fear. At that time Antalas sent to the Emperor Justinian a letter, which set forth the following:

"That I am a slave of thy empire not even I myself would deny, but the Moors, having suffered unholy treatment at the hands of Solomon in time of peace, have taken up arms under the most severe constraint, not lifting them against thee, but warding off our personal enemy; and this is especially true of me. For he not only decided to deprive me of the maintenance, which Belisarius long before specified and thou didst grant, but he also killed my own brother, although he had no wrongdoing to charge against him. We have therefore taken vengeance upon him who wronged us. And if it is thy will that the Moors be in subjection to thy empire and serve it in all things as they are accustomed to do, command Sergius, the nephew of Solomon, to depart from here and return to thee, and send another general to Libya. For thou wilt not be lacking in men of discretion and more worthy than Sergius in every way; for as long as this man commands thy army, it is impossible for peace to be established between the Romans and the Moors."

Such was the letter written by Antalas. But the emperor, even after reading these things and learning the common enmity of all toward Sergius, was still unwilling to remove him from his office, out of respect for the virtues of Solomon and especially the manner of his death. Such, then, was the course of these events.

But Solomon, the brother of Sergius, who was supposed to have disappeared from the world together with his uncle Solomon, was forgotten by his brother and by the rest as well; for no one had learned that he was alive. But the Moors, as it happened, had taken him alive, since he was very young; and they enquired of him who he was. And he said that he was a Vandal by birth, and a slave of Solomon. He said, moreover, that he had a friend, a physician, Pegasius by name, in the city of Laribus near by, who would purchase him by giving ransom. So the Moors came up close to the fortifications of the city and called Pegasius and displayed Solomon to him, and asked whether it was his pleasure to purchase the man. And since he agreed to purchase him, they sold Solomon to him for fifty pieces of gold. But upon getting inside the fortifications, Solomon taunted the Moors as having been deceived by him, a mere lad; for he said that he was no other than Solomon, the son of Bacchus and nephew of Solomon. And the Moors, being deeply stung by what had happened, and counting it a terrible thing that, while having a strong security for the conduct of Sergius and the Romans, they had relinquished it so carelessly, came to Laribus and laid siege to the place, in order to capture Solomon with the city. And the besieged, in terror at being shut in by the barbarians, for they had not even carried in provisions, as it happened, opened negotiations with the Moors, proposing that upon receiving a great sum of money they should straightway abandon the siege. Whereupon the barbarians, thinking that they could never take the city by force, for the Moors are not at all practised in the storming of walls, and at the same time not knowing that provisions were scarce for the besieged, welcomed their words, and when they had received three thousand pieces of gold, they abandoned the siege, and all the Leuathae retired homeward.

## XXIII

But Antalas and the army of the Moors were gathering again in Byzacium and Stotzas was with them, having some few soldiers and Vandals. And John, the son of Sisiniolus, being earnestly entreated by the Libyans, gathered an army and marched against them. Now Himerius, the Thracian, was commander of the troops in Byzacium, and at that time he was ordered by John to bring with him all the troops there, together with the commanders of each detachment, and come to a place called Menephesse, which is in Byzacium, and join his force there. But later, upon hearing that the enemy were encamped there, John wrote to Himerius telling what had happened and directing him to unite with his forces at another place, that they might not go separately, but all together, to encounter the enemy. But by some chance those who had this letter, making use of another road, were quite unable to find Himerius, and he together with his army, coming upon the camp of the enemy, fell into their hands. Now there was in this Roman army a certain youth, Severianus, son of Asiaticus, a Phoenician and a native of Emesa, commanding a detachment of horse. This man alone, together with the soldiers under him, fifty in number, engaged with the enemy. And for some time they held out, but later, being overpowered by the great multitude, they ran to the top of a hill in the neighbourhood on which there was also a fort, but one which offered no security. For this reason they surrendered themselves to their opponents when they ascended the hill to attack them. And the Moors killed neither him nor any of the soldiers, but they made prisoners of the whole force; and Himerius they kept under guard, and handed over his soldiers to Stotzas, since they agreed with great readiness to march with the rebels against the Romans; Himerius, however, they threatened with death, if he should not carry out their commands. And they commanded him to put into their hands by some device the city of Hadrumetum on the sea. And since he declared that he was willing, they went with him against Hadrumetum. And upon coming near the city, they sent Himerius a little in advance with some of the soldiers of Stotzas, dragging along, as it seemed, some Moors in chains, and they themselves followed behind. And they directed Himerius to say to those in command of the gates of the city that the emperor's army had won a decisive victory, and that John would come very soon, bringing an innumerable multitude of Moorish captives; and when in this manner the gates had been opened to them, he was to get inside the fortifications together with those who went with him. And he carried out these instructions. And the citizens of Hadrumetum, being deceived in this way (for they could not distrust the commander of all the troops in Byzacium), opened wide the gates and received the enemy. Then, indeed, those who had entered with Himerius drew their swords and would not allow the guards there to shut the gates again, but straightway received the whole army of the Moors into the city. And the barbarians, after plundering it and establishing there some few guards, departed. And of the Romans who had been captured some few escaped and came to Carthage, among whom were Severianus and Himerius. For it was not difficult for those who wished it to make their escape from Moors. And many also, not at all unwillingly, remained with Stotzas.

Not long after this one of the priests, Paulus by name, who had been appointed to take charge of the sick, in conferring with some of the nobles, said: "I myself shall journey to Carthage and I am hopeful that I shall return quickly with an army, and it will be your care to receive the emperor's forces into the city." So they attached some ropes to him and let him down by night from the fortifications, and he, coming to the sea-shore and happening upon a fishing-vessel which was thereabouts, won over the masters of this boat by great sums of money and sailed off to Carthage. And when he had landed there and come into the presence of Sergius, he told the whole story and asked him to give him a considerable army in order to recover Hadrumetum. And since this by no means pleased Sergius, inasmuch as the army in Carthage was not great, the priest begged him to give him some few soldiers, and receiving not more than eighty men, he formed the following plan. He collected a large number of boats and skiffs and embarked on them many sailors and Libyans also, clad in the garments which the Roman soldiers are accustomed to wear. And setting off with the whole fleet, he sailed at full speed straight for Hadrumetum. And when he had come close to it, he sent some men stealthily and declared to the notables of the city that Germanus, the emperor's nephew, had recently come to Carthage, and had sent a very considerable army to the citizens of Hadrumetum. And he bade them take courage at this and open for them one small gate that night. And they carried out his orders. Thus Paulus with his followers got inside the fortifications, and he slew all the enemy and recovered Hadrumetum for the emperor; and the rumour about Germanus, beginning there, went even to Carthage. And the Moors, as well as Stotzas and his followers, upon hearing this, at first became terrified and went off in flight to the extremities of Libya, but later, upon learning the truth, they counted it a terrible thing that they, after sparing all the citizens of Hadrumetum, had suffered such things at their hands. For this reason they made raids everywhere and wrought unholy deeds upon the Libyans, sparing no one whatever his age, and the land became at that time for the most part depopulated. For of the Libyans who had been left some fled into the cities and some to Sicily and the other islands. But almost all the notables came to Byzantium, among whom was Paulus also, who had recovered Hadrumetum for the emperor. And the Moors with still less fear, since no one came out against them, were plundering everything, and with them Stotzas, who was now powerful. For many Roman soldiers were following him, some who had come as deserters, and others who had been in the beginning captives but now remained with him of their own free will. And John, who was indeed a man of some reputation among the Moors, was remaining quiet because of the extreme hostility he had conceived against Sergius.

XXIV

At this time the emperor sent to Libya, with some few soldiers, another general, Areobindus, a man of the senate and of good birth, but not at all skilled in matters of warfare. And he sent with him Athanasius, a prefect, who had come recently from Italy, and some few Armenians led by Artabanes and John, sons of John, of the line of the Arsacidae,[66] who had recently left the Persian army and as deserters had come back to the Romans, together with the other Armenians. And with Areobindus was his sister and Prejecta, his wife, who was the daughter of Vigilantia, the sister of the Emperor Justinian. The emperor, however, did not recall Sergius, but commanded both him and Areobindus to be generals of Libya, dividing the country and the detachments of soldiers between them. And he enjoined upon Sergius to carry on the war against the barbarians in Numidia, and upon Areobindus to direct his operations constantly against the Moors in Byzacium. And when this expedition lauded at Carthage, Sergius departed forthwith for Numidia with his own army, and Areobindus, upon learning that Antalas and Stotzas were encamped near the city of Siccaveneria, which is three days' journey distant from Carthage, commanded John, the son of Sisiniolus, to go against them, choosing out whatever was best of the army; and he wrote to Sergius to unite with the forces of John, in order that they might all with one common force engage with the enemy. Now Sergius decided to pay no heed to the message and have nothing to do with this affair, and John with a small army was compelled to engage with an innumerable host of the enemy. And there had always been great enmity between him and Stotzas, and each one used to pray that he might become the slayer of the other before departing from the world. At that time, accordingly, as soon as the fighting was about to come to close quarters, both rode out from their armies and came against each other. And John drew his bow, and, as Stotzas was still advancing, made a successful shot and hit him in the right groin, and Stotzas, mortally wounded, fell there, not yet dead, but destined to survive this wound only a little time. And all came up immediately, both the Moorish army and those who followed Stotzas, and placing Stotzas with little life in him against a tree, they advanced upon their enemy with great fury; and since they were far superior in numbers, they routed John and all the Romans with no difficulty. Then, indeed, they say, John remarked that death had now a certain sweetness for him, since his prayer regarding Stotzas had reached fulfilment. And there was a steep place near by, where his horse stumbled and threw him off. And as he was trying to leap upon the horse again, the enemy caught and killed him, a man who had shown himself great both in reputation and in valour. And Stotzas learned this and then died, remarking only that now it was most sweet to die. In this battle John, the Armenian, brother of Artabanes, also died, after making a display of valorous deeds against the enemy. And the emperor, upon hearing this, was very deeply grieved because of the valour of John; and thinking it inexpedient for the two generals to administer the province, he immediately recalled Sergius and sent him to Italy with an army, and gave over the whole power of Libya to Areobindus.

## XXV

And two months after Sergius had departed from there, Gontharis essayed to set up a tyranny in the following manner. He himself, as it happened, was commanding the troops in Numidia and spending his time there for that reason, but he was secretly treating with the Moors that they might march against Carthage. Forthwith, therefore, an army of the enemy, having been gathered into one place from Numidia and Byzacium, went with great zeal against Carthage. And the Numidians were commanded by Coutzinas and Iaudas, and the men of Byzacium by Antalas. And with him was also John, the tyrant, and his followers; for the mutineers, after the death of Stotzas, had set him up as ruler over themselves. And when Areobindus learned of their attack, he summoned to Carthage a number of the officers with their men, and among them Gontharis. And he was joined also by Artabanes and the Armenians. Areobindus, accordingly, bade Gontharis lead the whole army against the enemy. And Gontharis, though he had promised to serve him zealously in the war, proceeded to act as follows. One of his servants, a Moor by birth and a cook by trade, he commanded to go to the enemy's camp, and to make it appear to all others that he had run away from his master, but to tell Antalas secretly that Gontharis wished to share with him the rule of Libya. So the cook carried out these directions, and Antalas heard the word gladly, but made no further reply than to say that worthy enterprises are not properly brought to pass among men by cooks. When this was heard by Gontharis, he immediately sent to Antalas one of his body-guards, Ulitheus by name, whom he had found especially trustworthy in his service, inviting him to come as close as possible to Carthage. For, if this were done, he promised him to put Areobindus out of the way. So Ulitheus without the knowledge of the rest of the barbarians made an agreement with Antalas that he, Antalas, should rule Byzacium, having half the possessions of Areobindus and taking with him fifteen hundred Roman soldiers, while Gontharis should assume the dignity of king, holding the power over Carthage and the rest of Libya. And after settling these matters he returned to the Roman camp, which they had made entirely in front of the circuit-wall, distributing among themselves the guarding of each gate. And the barbarians not long afterwards proceeded straight for Carthage in great haste, and they made camp and remained in the place called Decimum.[67] And departing from there on the following day, they were moving forward. But some of the Roman army encountered them, and engaging with them unexpectedly, slew a small number of the Moors. But these were straightway called back by Gontharis, who rebuked them for acting with reckless daring and for being willing to give the Romans foreknowledge of the danger into which they were thrown.

But in the meantime Areobindus sent to Coutzinas secretly and began to treat with him with regard to turning traitor. And Coutzinas promised him that, as soon as they should begin the action, he would turn against Antalas and the Moors of Byzacium. For the Moors keep faith neither with any other men nor with each other. This Areobindus reported to Gontharis. And he, wishing to frustrate the enterprise by having it postponed, advised Areobindus by no means to have faith in Coutzinas, unless he should receive from him his children as hostages. So Areobindus and Coutzinas, constantly sending secret messages to each other, were busying themselves with the plot against Antalas. And Gontharis sent Ulitheus once more and made known to Antalas what was being done. And he decided not to make any charges against Coutzinas nor did he allow him to know that he had discovered the plot, nor indeed did he disclose anything of what had been agreed upon by himself and Gontharis. But though enemies and hostile at heart to one another, they were arrayed together with treacherous intent, and each of them was marching with the other against his own particular friend. With such purposes Coutzinas and Antalas were leading the Moorish army against Carthage. And Gontharis was intending to kill Areobindus, but, in order to avoid the appearance of aiming at sole power, he wished to do this secretly in battle, in order that it might seem that the plot had been made by others against the general, and that he had been compelled by the Roman army to assume command over Libya. Accordingly he circumvented Areobindus by deceit, and persuaded him to go out against the enemy and engage with them, now that they had already come close to Carthage. He decided, therefore, that on the following day he would lead the whole army against the enemy at sunrise. But Areobindus, being very inexperienced in this matter and reluctant besides, kept holding back for no good reason. For while considering how he should put on his equipment of arms and armour, and making the other preparations for the sally, he wasted the greatest part of the day. He accordingly put off the engagement to the following day and remained quiet. But Gontharis, suspecting that he had hesitated purposely, as being aware of what was being done, decided openly to accomplish the murder of the general and make his attempt at the tyranny.

XXVI

And on the succeeding day he proceeded to act as follows. Opening wide the gates where he himself kept guard, he placed huge rocks under them, that no one might be able easily to shut them, and he placed armoured men with bows in their hands about the parapet in great numbers, and he himself, having put on his breastplate, took his stand between the gates. And his purpose in doing this was not that he might receive the Moors into the city; for the Moors, being altogether fickle, are suspicious of all men. And it is not unnatural that they are so; for whoever is by nature treacherous toward his neighbours is himself unable to trust anyone at all, but he is compelled to be suspicious of all men, since he estimates the character of his neighbour by his own mind. For this reason, then, Gontharis did not hope that even the Moors would trust him and come inside the circuit-wall, but he made this move in order that Areobindus, falling into great fear, might straightway rush off in flight, and, abandoning Carthage as quickly as he could, might betake himself to Byzantium. And he would have been right in his expectation had not winter come on just then and frustrated his plan. [544-545 A.D.] And Areobindus, learning what was being done, summoned Athanasius and some of the notables. And Artabanes also came to him from the camp with two others and he urged Areobindus neither to lose heart nor to give way to the daring of Gontharis, but to go against him instantly with all his men and engage him in battle, before any further trouble arose. At first, then, Areobindus sent to Gontharis one of his friends, Phredas by name, and commanded him to test the other's purpose. And when Phredas returned and reported that Gontharis by no means denied his intention of seizing the supreme power, he purposed immediately to go against him arrayed for battle.

But in the meantime Gontharis slandered Areobindus to the soldiers, saying that he was a coward and not only possessed with fear of the enemy, but at the same time quite unwilling to give them, his soldiers, their pay, and that he was planning to run away with Anastasius and that they were about to sail very soon from Mandracium[68], in order that the soldiers, fighting both with hunger and with the Moors, might be destroyed; and he enquired whether it was their wish to arrest both and keep them under guard. For thus he hoped either that Areobindus, perceiving the tumult, would turn to flight, or that he would be captured by the soldiers and ruthlessly put to death. Moreover he promised that he himself would advance to the soldiers money of his own, as much as the government owed them. And they were approving his words and were possessed with great wrath against Areobindus, but while this was going on Areobindus together with Artabanes and his followers came there. And a battle took place on the parapet and below about the gate where Gontharis had taken his stand, and neither side was worsted. And all were about to gather from the camps, as many as were well disposed to the emperor, and capture the mutineers by force. For Gontharis had not as yet deceived all, but the majority remained still uncorrupted in mind. But Areobindus, seeing then for the first time the killing of men (for he had not yet, as it happened, become acquainted with this sight), was terror-stricken and, turning coward, fled, unable to endure what he saw.

Now there is a temple inside the fortifications of Carthage hard by the sea-shore, the abode of men who are very exact in their practice of religion, whom we have always been accustomed to call "monks"; this temple had been built by Solomon not long before, and he had surrounded it with a wall and rendered it a very strong fortress. And Areobindus, fleeing for refuge, rushed into the monastery, where he had already sent his wife and sister. Then Artabanes too ran away, and all the rest withdrew from Carthage as each one could. And Gontharis, having taken the city by assault, with the mutineers took possession of the palace, and was already guarding both the gates and the harbour most carefully. First, then, he summoned Athanasius, who came to him without delay, and by using much flattery Athanasius made it appear that what had been done pleased him exceedingly. And after this Gontharis sent the priest of the city and commanded Areobindus, after receiving pledges, to come to the palace, threatening that he would besiege him if he disobeyed and would not again give him pledges of safety, but would use every means to capture and put him to death. So the priest, Reparatus, stoutly declared to Areobindus that in accordance with the decision of Gontharis he would swear that no harm would come to him from Gontharis, telling also what he had threatened in case he did not obey. But Areobindus became afraid and agreed that he would follow the priest immediately, if the priest, after performing the rite of the sacred bath[69] in the usual manner, should swear to him by that rite and then give him pledges for his safety. So the priest did according to this. And Areobindus without delay followed him, clad in a garment which was suitable neither for a general nor for anyone else in military service, but altogether appropriate to a slave or one of private station; this garment the Romans call "casula"[70] in the Latin tongue. And when they came near the palace, he took in his hands the holy scriptures from the priest, and so went before Gontharis. And falling prone he lay there a long time, holding out to him the suppliant olive-branch and the holy scriptures, and with him was the child which had been counted worthy of the sacred bath by which the priest had given him the pledge, as has been told. And when, with difficulty, Gontharis had raised him to his feet, he enquired of Gontharis in the name of all things holy whether his safety was secure. And Gontharis now bade him most positively to be of good cheer, for he would suffer no harm at his hands, but on the following day would be gone from Carthage with his wife and his possessions. Then he dismissed the priest Reparatus, and bade Areobindus and Athanasius dine with him in the palace. And during the dinner he honoured Areobindus, inviting him to take his place first on the couch; but after the dinner he did not let him go, but compelled him to sleep in a chamber alone; and he sent there Ulitheus with certain others to assail him. And while he was wailing and crying aloud again and again and speaking many entreating words to them to move them to pity, they slew him. Athanasius, however, they spared, passing him by, I suppose, on account of his advanced age.

## XXVII

And on the following day Gontharis sent the head of Areobindus to Antalas, but decided to deprive him of the money and of the soldiers. Antalas, therefore, was outraged, because he was not carrying out anything of what had been agreed with him, and at the same time, upon considering what Gontharis had sworn and what he had done to Areobindus, he was incensed. For it did not seem to him that one who had disregarded such oaths would ever be faithful either to him or to anyone else at all. So after considering the matter long with himself, he was desirous of submitting to the Emperor Justinian; for this reason, then, he marched back. And learning that Marcentius, who commanded the troops in Byzacium, had fled to one of the islands which lie off the coast, he sent to him, and telling him the whole story and giving pledges, persuaded him by kind words to come to him. And Marcentius remained with Antalas in the camp, while the soldiers who were on duty in Byzacium, being well disposed to the emperor, were guarding the city of Hadrumetum. But the soldiers of Stotzas, being not less than a thousand, perceiving what was being done, went in great haste, with John leading them, to Gontharis; and he gladly received them into the city. Now there were five hundred Romans and about eighty Huns, while all the rest were Vandals. And Artabanes, upon receiving pledges, went up to the palace with his Armenians, and promised to serve the tyrant according to his orders. But secretly he was purposing to destroy Gontharis, having previously communicated this purpose to Gregorius, his nephew, and to Artasires, his body-guard. And Gregorius, urging him on to the undertaking, spoke as follows:

"Artabanes, the opportunity is now at hand for you, and you alone, to win the glory of Belisarius, nay more, even to surpass that glory by far. For he came here, having received from the emperor a most formidable army and great sums of money, having officers accompanying him and advisers in great numbers, and a fleet of ships whose like we have never before heard tell of, and numerous cavalry, and arms, and everything else, to put it in a word, prepared for him in a manner worthy of the Roman empire. And thus equipped he won back Libya for the Romans with much toil. But all these achievements have so completely come to naught, that they are, at this moment, as if they had never been, except indeed, that there is at present left to the Romans from the victory of Belisarius the losses they have suffered in lives and in money, and, in addition, that they are no longer able even to guard the good things they won. But the winning back of all these things for the emperor now depends upon the courage and judgment and right hand of you alone. Therefore consider that you are of the house of the Arsacidae by ancient descent, and remember that it is seemly for men of noble birth to play the part of brave men always and in all places. Now many remarkable deeds have been performed by you in behalf of freedom. For when you were still young, you slew Acacius,[71] the ruler of the Armenians, and Sittas,[72] the general of the Romans, and as a result of this becoming known to the king Chosroes, you campaigned with him against the Romans. And since you have reached so great a station that it devolves upon you not to allow the Roman power to lie subject to a drunken dog, show at this time that it was by reason of noble birth and a valorous heart that at the former time, good sir, you performed those deeds; and I as well as Artasires here will assist you in everything, so far as we have the power, in accordance with your commands."

So spoke Gregorius; and he excited the mind of Artabanes still more against the tyrant. But Gontharis, bringing out the wife and the sister of Areobindus from the fortress, compelled them to remain at a certain house, showing them no insult by any word or deed whatsoever, nor did they have provisions in any less measure than they needed, nor were they compelled to say or to do anything except, indeed, that Prejecta was forced to write to her uncle[73] that Gontharis was honouring them exceedingly and that he was altogether guiltless of the murder of her husband, and that the base deed had been done by Ulitheus, Gontharis by no means approving. And Gontharis was persuaded to do this by Pasiphilus, a man who had been foremost among the mutineers in

Byzacium, and had assisted Gontharis very greatly in his effort to establish the tyranny. For Pasiphilus maintained that, if he should do this, the emperor would marry the young woman to him, and in view of his kinship with her would give also a, dowry of a large sum of money. And Gontharis commanded Artabanes to lead the army against Antalas and the Moors in Byzacium. For Coutzinas, having quarrelled with Antalas, had separated from him openly and allied himself with Gontharis; and he gave Gontharis his son and his mother as hostages. So the army, under the leadership of Artabanes, proceeded immediately against Antalas. And with Artabanes was John also, the commander of the mutineers of Stotzas, and Ulitheus, the body-guard of Gontharis; and there were Moors also following him, led by Coutzinas. And after passing by the city of Hadrumetum, they came upon their opponents somewhere near there, and making a camp a little apart from the enemy, they passed the night. And on the day after that John and Ulitheus, with a detachment of the army, remained there, while Artabanes and Coutzinas led their army against their opponents. And the Moors under Antalas did not withstand their attack and rushed off in flight. But Artabanes of a sudden wilfully played the coward, and turning his standard about marched off towards the rear. For this reason Ulitheus was purposing to kill him when he came into the camp. But Artabanes, by way of excusing himself, said he feared lest Marcentius, coming to assist the enemy from the city of Hadrumetum, where he then happened to be, would do his forces irreparable harm; but Gontharis, he said, ought to march against the enemy with the whole army. And at first he considered going to Hadrumetum with his followers and uniting with the emperor's forces. But after long deliberation it seemed to him better to put Gontharis out of the world and thus free both the emperor and Libya from a difficult situation. Returning, accordingly, to Carthage, he reported to the tyrant that he would need a larger army to meet the enemy. And Gontharis, after conferring with Pasiphilus, consented, indeed, to equip his whole army, but purposed to place a guard in Carthage, and in person to lead the army against the enemy. Each day, therefore, he was destroying many men toward whom he felt any suspicion, even though groundless. And he gave orders to Pasiphilus, whom he was intending to appoint in charge of the garrison of Carthage, to kill all the Greeks[74] without any consideration.

XXVIII

And after arranging everything else in the very best way, as it seemed to him, Gontharis decided to entertain his friends at a banquet, with the intention of making his departure on the following day. And in a room where there were in readiness three couches which had been there from ancient times, he made the banquet. So he himself reclined, as was natural, upon the first couch, where were also Athanasius and Artabanes, and some of those known to Gontharis, and Peter, a Thracian by birth, who had previously been a body-guard of Solomon. And on both the other couches were the first and noblest of the Vandals. John, however, who commanded the mutineers of Stotzas; was entertained by Pasiphilus in his own house, and each of the other leaders wherever it suited the several friends of Gontharis to entertain them. Artabanes, accordingly, when he was bidden to this banquet, thinking that this occasion furnished him a suitable opportunity for the murder of the tyrant, was planning to carry out his purpose. He therefore disclosed the matter to Gregorius and to Artasires and three other body-guards, bidding the body-guards get inside the hall with their swords (for when commanders are entertained at a banquet it is customary for their body-guards to stand behind them), and after getting inside to make an attack suddenly, at whatever moment should seem to them most suitable; and Artasires was to strike the first blow. At the same time he directed Gregorius to pick out a large number of the most daring of the Armenians and bring them to the palace, carrying only their swords in their hands (for it is not lawful for the escort of officers in a city to be armed with anything else), and leaving these men in the vestibule, to come inside with the body-guards; and he was to tell the plan to no one of them, but to make only this explanation, that he was suspicious of Gontharis, fearing that he had called Artabanes to this banquet to do him harm, and therefore wished that they should stand beside the soldiers of Gontharis who had been stationed there on guard, and giving the appearance of indulging in some play, they were to take hold of the shields which these guards carried, and waving them about and otherwise moving them keep constantly turning them up and down; and if any tumult or shouting took place within, they were to take up these very shields and come to the rescue on the run. Such were the orders which Artabanes gave, and Gregorius proceeded to put them into execution. And Artasires devised the following plan: he cut some arrows into two parts and placed them on the wrist of his left arm, the sections reaching to his elbow. And after binding them very carefully with straps, he laid over them the sleeve of his tunic. And he did this in order that, if anyone should raise his sword over him and attempt to strike him, he might avoid the chance of suffering serious injury; for he had only to thrust his left arm in front of him, and the steel would break off as it crashed upon the wood, and thus his body could not be reached at any point.

With such purpose, then, Artasires did as I have said. And to Artabanes he spoke as follows: "As for me, I have hopes that I shall prove equal to the undertaking and shall not hesitate, and also that I shall touch the body of Gontharis with this sword; but as for what will follow, I am unable to say whether God in His anger against the tyrant will co-operate with me in this daring deed, or whether, avenging some sin of mine, He will stand against me there and be an obstacle in my way. If, therefore, you see that the tyrant is not wounded in a vital spot, do you kill me with my sword without the least hesitation, so that I may not be tortured by him into saying that it was by your will that I rushed into the undertaking, and thus not only perish myself most shamefully, but also be compelled against my will to destroy you as well." And after Artasires had spoken such words he too, together with Gregorius and one of the body-guards, entered the room where the couches were and took his stand behind Artabanes. And the rest, remaining by the guards, did as they had been commanded.

So Artasires, when the banquet had only just begun, was purposing to set to work, and he was already touching the hilt of his sword. But Gregorius prevented him by saying in the Armenian tongue that Gontharis was still wholly himself, not having as yet drunk any great quantity of wine. Then Artasires groaned and said: "My good fellow, how fine a heart I have for the deed, and now you have for the moment wrongfully hindered me!" And as the drinking went on, Gontharis, who by now was thoroughly saturated with wine, began to give portions of the food to the body-guards, yielding to a generous mood. And they, upon receiving these portions, went outside the building immediately and were about to eat them, leaving beside Gontharis only three body-guards, one of whom happened to be Ulitheus. And Artasires also started to go out in order to taste the morsels with the rest. But just then a kind of fear came over him lest, when he should wish to draw his sword, something might prevent him. Accordingly, as soon as he got outside, he secretly threw away the sheath of the sword, and taking it naked under his arm, hidden by his cloak, he rushed in to Gontharis, as if to say something without the knowledge of the others. And Artabanes, seeing this, was in a fever of excitement, and became exceedingly anxious by reason of the surpassing magnitude of the issue at stake; he began to move his head, the colour of his countenance changed repeatedly, and he seemed to have become altogether like one inspired, on account of the greatness of the undertaking. And Peter, upon seeing this, understood what was being done, but he did not disclose it to any of the others, because, being well disposed to the emperor, he was exceedingly pleased by what was going on. And Artasires, having come close to the tyrant, was pushed by one of the servants, and as he retreated a little to the rear, the servant observed that his sword was bared and cried out saying: "What is this, my excellent fellow?" And Gontharis, putting his hand to his right ear, and turning his face, looked at him. And Artasires struck him with his sword as he did so, and cut off a piece of his scalp together with his fingers. And Peter cried out and exhorted Artasires to kill the most unholy of all men. And Artabanes, seeing Gontharis leaping to his feet (for he reclined close to him), drew a two-edged dagger which hung by his thigh, a rather large one, and thrusting it into the tyrant's left side clean up to the hilt, left it there. And the tyrant none the less tried to leap up, but having received a mortal wound, he fell where he was. Ulitheus then brought his sword down upon Artasires as if to strike him over the head; but he held his left arm above his head, and thus profited by his own idea in the moment of greatest need. For since Ulitheus' sword had its edge turned when it struck the sections of arrows on his arm, he himself was unscathed, and he killed Ulitheus with no difficulty. And Peter and Artabanes, the one seizing the sword of Gontharis and the other that of Ulitheus who had fallen, killed on the spot those of the body-guards who remained. Thus there arose, as was natural, an exceedingly great tumult and confusion. And when this was perceived by those of the Armenians who were standing by the tyrant's guards, they immediately picked up the shields according to the plan which had been arranged with them, and went on the run to the banquet-room. And they slew all the Vandals and the friends of Gontharis, no one resisting.

Then Artabanes enjoined upon Athanasius to take charge of the money in the palace: for all that had been left by Areobindus was there. And when the guards learned of the death of Gontharis, straightway many arrayed themselves with the Armenians; for the most of them were of the household of Areobindus. With one accord, therefore, they proclaimed the Emperor Justinian triumphant. And the cry, coming forth from a multitude of men, and being, therefore, an exceedingly mighty sound, was strong enough to reach the greater part of the city. Wherefore those who were well-disposed to the emperor leaped into the houses of the mutineers and straightway killed them, some while enjoying sleep, others while taking food, and still others while they were awe-struck with fear and in terrible perplexity. And among these was Pasiphilus, but not John, for he with some of the Vandals fled to the sanctuary. To these Artabanes gave pledges, and making them rise from there, sent them to Byzantium, and having thus recovered the city for the emperor, he continued to guard it. And the murder of the tyrant took place on the thirty-sixth day of the tyranny, in the nineteenth year of the reign of the Emperor Justinian. [545-546 A.D.]

And Artabanes won great fame for himself from this deed among all men. And straightway Prejecta, the wife of Areobindus, rewarded him with great sums of money, and the emperor appointed him general of all Libya. But not long after this Artabanes entreated the emperor to summon him to Byzantium, and the emperor fulfilled his request. And having summoned Artabanes, he appointed John, the brother of Pappus, sole general of Libya. And this John, immediately upon arriving in Libya, had an engagement with Antalas and the Moors in Byzacium, and conquering them in battle, slew many; and he wrested from these barbarians all the standards of Solomon, and sent them to the emperor, standards which they had previously secured as plunder, when Solomon had been taken from the world.[75] And the rest of the Moors he drove as far as possible from the Roman territory. But at a later time the Leuathae came again with a great army from the country about Tripolis to Byzacium, and united with the forces of Antalas. And when John went to meet this army, he was defeated in the engagement, and losing many of his men, fled to Laribus. And then indeed the enemy, overrunning the whole country there as far as Carthage, treated in a terrible manner those Libyans who fell in their way. But not long afterward John collected those of the soldiers who had survived, and drawing into alliance with him many Moors and especially those under Coutzinas, came to battle with the enemy and unexpectedly routed them. And the Romans, following them up as they fled in complete disorder, slew a great part of them, while the rest escaped to the confines of Libya. Thus it came to pass that those of the Libyans who survived, few as they were in number and exceedingly poor, at last and after great toil found some peace.

FOOTNOTES

[1] The vexillum praetorium carried by the cavalry of the imperial guard, IV. x. 4 below; cf. Lat. pannum.

[2] See III. xxiv. 1.

[3] "Auxiliaries"; see Book III. xi. 3 and note.

[4] Chap. i. 3.

[5] Chap. i. 3.

[6] Now Bona; it was the home and burial-place of St. Augustine.

[7] The Eruli, or Heruli, were one of the wildest and most corrupt of the barbarian tribes. They came from beyond the Danube. On their origin, practices, and character, see VI. xiv.

[8] The Greek implies that the Tuscan Sea was stormy, like the Adriatic. The Syrtes farther east had a bad reputation.

[9] About twelve miles west of Algiers, originally Iol, now Cherchel; named after Augustus.

[10] See III. i. 6 and note.

[11] See III. i. 18.

[12] Book III. ix. 9.

[13] See III. x. 23

[14] Lilybaeum had been ceded to the Vandals by Theoderic as dower of his sister Amalafrida on her marriage to Thrasamund, the African king (III. viii. 13).

[15] "Friendship" and "hostility" refer to the present relations between Justinian and the Goths and what they may become.

[16] Amalasountha.

[17] The correspondence between Queen Amalasountha and Justinian is given in V. iii. 17.

[18] In Latin serica, "silk," as coming from the Chinese (Seres).

[19] Cf. Thucydides' description of the huts in which the Athenians lived during the great plague.

[20] Pharas and the other Eruli.

[21] Cf. ch. vi. 4.

[22] "Auxiliaries"; see Book III. xi. 3.

[23] i.e. there in Africa, as successor to the throne of the Vandal kings.

[24] Book III. xxv. 2-4.

[25] Examples of the Roman system have come to light in Egyptian papyri: cf. the declarations of personal property, [Greek: apographai], Pap. Lond., I., p. 79; Flinders Petrie Pap., III., p. 200, ed. Mahaffy and Smyly.

[26] Since a triumph was granted only to an imperator, after the establishment of the principate by Augustus all triumphs were celebrated in the name of the emperor himself, the victorious general receiving only the insignia triumphalia. The first general to refuse a triumph was Agrippa, after his campaign in Spain, about 550 years before Belisarius' triumph in Constantinople.

[27] The barriers (carceres), or starting-point for the racers, were at the open end of the hippodrome, the imperial box at the middle of the course at the right as one entered.

[28] Cf. Book III. v. 3; that was in A.D. 455. The spoliation of Jerusalem by Titus had taken place in A.D. 70.

[29] Ecclesiastes, i. 2.

[30] Not an actual "triumph," but a triumphal celebration of his inauguration as consul.

[31] The reference is to the old custom of distributing to the populace largesses (congiaria) of money or valuables on the occasion of events of interest to the imperial house, such as the emperor's assumption of the consular office, birthdays, etc. The first largess of this kind was made by Julius Caesar.

[32] Cf. Book IV. ii. 1.

[33] The Canaanites of the Old Testament.

[34] i.e., Clypea, or Aspis, now Kalibia, on the Carthaginian coast.

[35] i.e., from Tangier, opposite Cadiz, to Algiers. On Caesarea see IV. v. 5 and note.

[36] "On the borders of Mauretania" according to Procopius, De aedificiis, vi. 6. 18.

[37] Chap. x. 6.

[38] Book III. viii. 25, 26.

[39] The side toward the mountains; cf. § 20.

[40] In the late Empire the excubitores, 300 in number, constituted the select guard of the palace. Their commander, comes excubitorum, held high rank at court; cf. VIII. xxi. 1, where we are told that Belisarius held this position, and Arcana 6. 10, where Justin, afterwards emperor, is mentioned.

[41] Cf. chap. viii. 14. Procopius has explained in III. xi. 6 that Solomon was a eunuch.

[42] See III. viii. 5.

[43] A comes foedtratorum, mentioned in III. xi. 6.

[44] Book III. viii. 5.

[45] i.e. Clypea. Not the place mentioned in IV. x. 24.

[46] The region in the interior of Sardinia called Barbargia or Barbagia still preserves this name. But Procopius' explanation of the origin of the barbarian settlers there has not been generally accepted.

[47] Book III. xviii. 7 ff.

[48] IV. iv. 30 and note.

[49] Baptism was administered only during the fifty days between Easter and Pentecost. Justinian had forbidden the baptism of Arians.

[50] Cf. III. xi. 30.

[51] Cf. chap. xiv. 8.

[52] "Auxiliaries"; see Book III. xi. 3.

[53] More correctly Gadiaufala, now Ksar-Sbehi.

[54] Cirta, later named Constantina, now Constantine (Ksantina).

[55] John the Cappadocian, cf. I. xxiv. 11 ff.

[56] See Book III. xvii. 1 and note.

[57] Now Setif.

[58] Called Mastinas in IV. xiii. 19.

[59] Book IV. v. 5.

[60] Cyrenaica.

[61] Now Lebida.

[62] Cf. III. xxv. 4 ff.

[63] Book III. x. 22 ff.

[64] Book IV. xii. 30.

[65] A reference to his slaughter of the eighty notables, IV. xxi. 7, where, however, nothing is said of an oath sworn on the Gospels.

[66] Cf. Book II. iii. 32.

[67] Cf. Book III. xvii. 11, xxi. 23.

[68] The port of Carthage; see III. xx. 3.

[69] i.e. baptism.

[70] A garment with a cowl, like the cucullus.

[71] Cf. Book II. iii. 25.

[72] Cf. Book II. iii. 15.

[73] Justinian.

[74] A contemptuous term for "subjects of the emperor."

[75] See Book IV. xxi. 27.